ONE LAST TALK

ONE

**Why your truth matters
and how to speak it.**

LAST

PHILIP McKERNAN

TALK

ONE LAST TALK

Why Your Truth Matters and How to Speak It

ISBN   978-1-5445-0097-3 *Hardcover*
       978-1-5445-0096-6 *Ebook*

For Pauline, Maggie, and Charlie

Contents

How to Think about One Last Talk

BY TUCKER MAX

If you let it, this book will change your life.

But fair warning: you might not enjoy the process to get there.

I know I didn't like it. More than once, I wanted to quit. But I didn't, and I'm eternally grateful I kept going.

To understand what this book is about and how it can help you, you have to start with the man who wrote it: Philip McKernan.

When I first met Philip, I did not like him. Not at all.

We were both speaking at MasterMind Talks, an event for entrepreneurs. I went first, gave my speech, and did fine. Polite standing ovation, etc.

Then Philip spoke. He was supposed to speak for an hour. He went for an hour and a half.

But *no one cared*. Not even the organizer. They were all totally enraptured.

I was not. I've been doing public speaking a long time, and I wasn't fooled. To me, he was arrogant, defiant, aggressive, and contemptuous. But even worse...*he just pissed me off* (as I've come to realize, this is a very common reaction people have when they first meet him).

But I have to admit, the audience was enraptured for a reason: he was good. Whatever I thought of him as a person, the man could speak.

Even though we weren't competing for anything, I looked at him the same way you might look at an opponent; you can't actually like them, but you can recognize they're objectively good at what they do.

Later that day, we ended up talking. I started asking him questions. After all, I could play his game too. *Let's see how good he is.*

Tucker: "So, you're good at dealing with people's problems?"

Philip: "Well...uh, I've helped some people in the past."

Tucker: "Okay, here's what I think is going on with me: [fifteen minutes of a rambling, self-aggrandizing self-diagnosis]. So? What do you think?"

Philip: "That's a great intellectual understanding of your issues. I have nothing to add. But let me ask you a question: how do you feel?"

Tucker: "I feel great!"

Phillip: "Okay. Then why bring this up?"

Tucker: "Oh, you know...just wanna see if you have anything to add."

Philip: "If you feel great, then I'm sure you don't need my help. But in my experience, people with great intellectual understandings of their issues are often the ones with little to no emotional connection to them."

Veronica (my wife): "Yep, he's right. That's you."

To hell with them both!

Over the years that ensued, we spoke at or attended the same events several times, and I got to know Philip very well (which was much easier than I expected, because he's very likable one-on-one).

As I got to know him more, I also started to see him work with clients, many of whom were my friends. When I saw the impact he had on his clients, my feelings about him shifted.

I've seen hundreds of business coaches, CEO coaches, life coaches—every sort of coach there is. I think most of them are completely useless (in fact, I think quite a few are destructive).

But the first time I saw McKernan coach, I was blown away. He didn't have any of the attributes you would assume a good coach would have—except the most important: his method works.

When he coached, all the things I told myself that I didn't like about him—his cheekiness, his arrogance, his defiance—all disappeared. Instead, I saw a man who was 100 percent focused on the person he was helping, totally without ego. He approached each client from a genuine place of curiosity, humility, and service.

His coaching was, in a word, beautiful.

The difference is that most coaches or therapists like that are soft and cuddly and weak. He was not. At the same time he was in this service mindset, he also had a fierceness and a determination to actually get at the core of what was wrong.

I'd never personally seen this combination before—a coach who was deeply kind and caring and supportive, but also relentless, demanding, and unyielding.

It was like he loved his clients so much that he refused to let them hide from their truth.

I'll be honest: this also irked me. Understanding people and helping them see themselves clearly is something I consider myself good at. People ask me to help them with this stuff all the time. Yet McKernan did it in a way that was so much more effective.

So basically, people liked him more *and* he did a better job.

Screw him!

Eventually, I got past my immaturity and looked at what he was doing from a place of humble curiosity, and I was able to see the secrets of his coaching techniques. I'll tell you exactly what they are—but you're going to be let down. His techniques are actually easy to understand.

They are just very difficult for most people to implement (that includes me).

He doesn't try to guess what's in people's heads. He doesn't force things on people. He just creates a space for people to feel comfortable exploring their own emotions, and then he asks the questions necessary to get them to look deep in themselves and recognize what they already know is there. And he holds them accountable to what they find when they look within themselves.

Like I said: simple to explain, but hard to do.

And that sums up this book as well.

———

One Last Talk is very, very simple to explain. I can do it right now:

If you were about to die, what would you say before you go, and who would you say it to?

When I heard him explain this for the first time, I got chills immediately. I knew where he was going and what this meant, especially coming from him.

I've been around death a few times, and it always plays out

the same way: *when people know it's their time, everything they'd been keeping inside comes out.*

They finally face the hard pain they've been avoiding. They finally speak their truth. They finally say that thing that needs to be said to that person that so needs to hear it.

One Last Talk is about bringing this forward in time. It's about using the idea of death to create the urgency that people lack in facing their issues.

I honestly don't know of any psychological, moral, or emotional frame that is more powerful than that.

Even though I was impressed by the idea and honored when he asked me to give a talk, I didn't think *One Last Talk* would impact me all that much. I'm not the type to run from my issues, and I felt like I had done most of the hard work already—that I had faced my pain and had spoken my truths.

I spent four years in psychoanalysis, going four times a week. I spent a year and a half doing a different form of therapy. I meditate. I've done an immense amount of deep and difficult emotional work. The really, really hard work that is awful and painful. The work people don't want to do.

How much could this impact me after all this work I'd already done?

Quite a bit. And yes, it was painful.

But it was also liberating.

My full One Last Talk is on YouTube, but in short, I got up on stage and admitted that I have real problems emotionally connecting with my wife and kids.

That *sucked*.

It wasn't even admitting it to the world that was hard. Or even to my wife. For me, it was *admitting it to myself.*

I think this is difficult for many people, but it's one of those truths that no one's willing to admit because it's shameful. I still feel deeply ashamed as I sit here and write: "I have an incredible, wonderful wife and two beautiful, healthy kids—and *I have real problems loving them.*"

Who admits that? I didn't want to admit that!

But when I gave my One Last Talk, that was the truth that was staring me in the face, that I was not confronting, that I needed to speak.

I'm not going to tell you that One Last Talk is a replacement for therapy, or that One Last Talk is perfect, or that One Last Talk will solve all your problems, because none of that is true.

But if you approach this with real conviction and real sincerity, and you really try your best—you will change. For the better.

It happened to me. And I've seen it happen in dozens of others who've worked with McKernan or have gone through the One Last Talk process.

I could go on and on about how great this is, but the highest recommendation I know to give for something is not words—which is ironic, given that I'm a writer. No, I'm a big believer that if you want to really understand someone, *watch what they do*.

This is what I did for this book:

- I delivered a One Last Talk myself, which required weeks of dedicated time on my part, and lots of travel— which I *hate*.
- Of course, I had to actually face that truth and then speak it on stage, which was far harder than I thought it'd be.

- I personally spent hundreds of hours helping edit this book.
- I spent dozens of hours helping Philip and his team brainstorm about how to conceptualize One Last Talk beyond just in-person events.
- I asked Philip to let me write the introduction to this book, and then I wrote it.

Measured that way—by the amount of time I've dedicated to it—I think One Last Talk gets the highest endorsement I've ever given a book.

Why did I spend so much time on this when it is not my project and I didn't have to?

Because the message in this book is that important.

The way life works is that we all suffer traumas.

Something awful happens.

Or someone hurts us.

Or we get judged and shamed.

Or we hide part of ourselves, for any number of reasons.

Any number of other awful things can and will happen to us. After all, so much of life is pain and suffering.

This suffering is an inevitable part of life.

The question becomes, how do we deal with it? What do we do after the unavoidable trauma and the pain and the suffering?

The answer for most people—myself included—is that we run from that pain.

We do drugs, we sleep with lots of people, we make lots of money, we stay constantly busy. We do whatever is necessary to avoid the pain that will come from facing whatever hard truth there is in our life.

But all that does is bury the shame and the pain, and only for a little while. It doesn't go away. It's still there, and the longer you wait to surface it, the worse it is when it comes.

All I can tell you, as someone who's done this multiple times with multiple painful traumas in my life—when it comes to pain, the only way out is through it.

But *how*? How do you get through it?

It's not the only way, but One Last Talk is one of the best

frameworks I've experienced to help me get through my pain.

If you're in pain, if you have a truth to speak, if you want to get there but you need some help...this book will help you.

And it will change your life.

You just have to give your talk.

PART

WHY YOUR TRUTH MATTERS

ONE

1.1

Your Pain Has a Purpose: Philip McKernan

I was really fired up about my first big speaking event.

Five people showed up.

I remember getting on my high horse, thinking, *What is this? I didn't sign up for this.*

But then I caught myself and thought, *Who do you think you are? You've never even spoken before!*

I was there because somebody had overheard a conversation I was having and asked me to come speak to their group.

I pulled myself together and spoke as though there were 100,000 people in the audience. I gave my all.

Afterward, a guy came up to me and said, "I'd like you to come and speak to my students."

I immediately expected he was talking about a business school or a college.

No. He was a headmaster at a high school.

I thought, *No way am I going back to high school. I hated high school.*

He kept calling me, so eventually I said, "Okay, I'll come with two conditions. One, that the students actually want to be in the room. It has to be by choice. And two, that you pay something."

I think it was five dollars per person, and we gave it to charity. But there had to be some skin in the game.

I showed up, and there were 20 kids in the room. Out of 170 kids total in the school, 20 chose to show up.

Within the first minute and a half, I used the f-bomb. Straightaway, that changed the energy. It was on purpose. I wanted the kids to know that I wasn't like the other adults, that I wasn't going to lie to them or play to the niceties. I was going to be real.

A half hour in, I was sharing some of my story—I left out all the bits I didn't want to talk about, because I wanted to look cool. I wanted credibility in front of these students, and I thought highlighting the good parts of my life was the way to get it.

One student asked, "Where did you go to college, and what did you study?"

I remember looking at the young kid and thinking of a bullshit answer to give, something like, "I wanted to be an entrepreneur, so I didn't want to go to college."

But the truth is that *I did want to go to college*. Not for the education, but to go with my buddies. I would've gone if I'd done well enough on my exams.

When I looked into that kid's big brown eyes, I knew I couldn't lie to myself or to these kids. Not anymore.

I said, "I didn't go to college. Laugh if you want, but I'm dyslexic, and I failed pretty much every exam I ever sat for."

They didn't laugh.

The opposite happened.

At that moment, they stopped judging me.

There was an energy shift in the room. I could see it in their eyes. They saw me as human and weak and real. It was almost like all their skepticism left them, and they felt at ease with me and connected to me. They went from curiosity to love. Literally, there was love in their eyes.

They accepted me. For the first time, I felt accepted like never before, in any public forum.

For me, in that moment, the workshop pivoted. I let go of worrying about looking good. I stopped needing to sell them on who I was. It was possibly the best workshop I've ever run, even to this day.

This changed me. It helped me feel free to speak my truth without any judgment.

This was supposed to be a speech. But this changed it from a speech to a dialogue. I felt safe, so I opened it up, and asked them questions, and opened a dialogue with them.

And they, in turn, realized something: they didn't just have to sit there and listen. They could share their truth too. Suddenly, my speech became a dialogue as the students began to open up with me about their parents and the pressures they faced.

This was a pivotal moment in my life.

This is the moment when I stopped "telling my story." I stopped trying to look good.

Instead, I spoke my honest, painful truth.

This was the moment, despite my fears and my insecurities and my imperfections, I felt the world accepted me.

It wasn't always like this, of course. When I was 15 years old, I told my mom I wanted to get rid of my name, Philip.

I thought that by changing my name, I could get rid of my story, and even my identity. That's how deep the desire to escape ran inside of me. I felt like this because I was in a lot of pain. I was bullied and made fun of at school. I was judged for who I was.

I didn't feel accepted anywhere.

I tried everything I could to fit in, but nothing worked. I put on every mask I could find and tried to be anybody but Philip McKernan.

I did that for 37 years of my life.

I'm 44 now.

What took me 37 years to realize was that the work I really needed to do was on the past—the very past I was running from.

Here is my One Last Talk that explores some of this past I was running from.

PHILIP MCKERNAN'S ONE LAST TALK

"37, 38, 39, 40, 41."

I was sitting in school, in class, counting.

I would count until the pain stopped.

You might think that I was in a math class or geography class. Maybe counting all the countries in the world.

No.

I was counting the dandruff on the shoulder of the kid in front of me. I could see it so clearly because we wore dark uniforms to the high school I went to.

The reason I was counting the dandruff was that the shoulder represented the perfect line of sight. If I looked up high, the teacher would see me. If I was staring at the ground, the teacher would notice me. The shoulder allowed me to kind of look forward, so I wouldn't catch the eyes of my teacher.

This memory came rushing back to me about three years ago, the counting of dandruff on the student in front of me.

When I remembered this, shame and embarrassment overwhelmed me. Then I got past those emotions and to a place of curiosity.

I asked myself, "Well, why was I doing that?"

As I looked back at my life, I realized I was trying to stay sane in school.

You see, for me, school was a like a prison. I felt entrapped. I felt enclosed. I felt like I was behind bars. I was expected to learn and absorb copious amounts of information.

The problem was that I was dyslexic. And of course, no one in Ireland or my school knew what that was at the time.

Because no one knew what dyslexia was, the teachers thought I was just lazy, or stupid, or a combination of both. Quite a few teachers went out of their way to remind me of those things every single day. As though I didn't already feel inadequate in my own skin. I just couldn't comprehend why I couldn't do what every other kid could do so easily. But they reminded me.

I counted the dandruff to stay sane as I sat there for eight hours every single day, with this horrible feeling in my stomach and the looming threat that I would be asked to do the simplest of things—like read in front of my peers.

I remember one teacher actually looking at me one day and saying, "Why do you even come to school? Why do you even show up here? You amount to nothing in here." Then she pointed to the window, and said, "And you're going to amount to nothing out there."

Now, at the time, I actually believed that statement. I think when you hear something long enough and loud enough, especially from people who are authority figures, you start to believe it at a deeper level than perhaps you can even imagine yourself. You internalize it.

Their voice becomes the voice in your head.

I hoped and wanted for my home to be a refuge—where I could be myself and be nurtured. But not for me. Instead, I had an angry sibling who wasn't very happy in life, I believe, and took it out on me physically.

I didn't have a refuge. Not school, not home. Everything felt like it was against me.

I felt unsafe; I felt unseen; I felt unheard. I didn't even feel worthy of being seen or heard at all.

I remember getting my big break.

I remember coming into fourth year, I think it was. I went to a big rugby school. I wasn't the most athletic. I wasn't the biggest. But I was pretty fast. I remember hearing the rumor in the corridor that I had been picked to be on the junior rugby cup team.

This was huge.

I grew up in a very competitive environment at home. My two brothers were super competitive. Everything was a competition. If we got sunburned, it was about who got the most sunburned, etc. But the reality was that none of us had ever been picked for a team of any sort. This was big news.

When I walked up the corridor to see my name, and I turned,

I'll never forget the day. I walked past the teachers' study on the left, and there was this stale smell of old books and some tobacco.

I remember that smell so clearly.

The other thing I can remember is my heart, beating so hard.

As I walked up, there was just this noise, this crowd, buzzing around at the notice board because the rugby teams had just been announced. I remember turning the corner. I remember being met by a student—I can't remember who it was—with, "Jesus, McKernan, you're on the team."

I'd love to say they didn't say it with an element of surprise, but they were as shocked as I was, quite frankly.

We weren't picked on teams just based on pure skill. If you were academically inclined, you tended to get a bit of a nod. If you were very athletic, you tended to be given a break in academics. It just seemed that the more athletic or academic you were, the more accepted you were in school. I adhered to that. I believed in that. I wanted a part of that, I should say.

But I remember, as I approached the board, I actually kind of felt it may have been a joke. This was the only time my name was ever up in lights. It was the one time I was picked for something by my own individual effort, from my own individual skill. In other words, to some extent, I felt it was the first thing that I'd earned and had been recognized for.

As I approached the board, I saw my name.

My name was last on the list, but it was on the list, nonetheless.

"Oh my God, I'm on the junior rugby cup team. Holy shit. This is just incredible."

I tried to act cool. I tried to not make a big deal of it, because I kind of felt like maybe somebody was going to say, "It's only a joke." Or, "Oh, there's two Philip McKernans in the school. The other one got picked."

But no, it was real. I was on the team.

I remember going home, so excited, and sharing. My news wasn't met with great applause, though. Not that I necessarily wanted applause, but I think I wanted and desired to be recognized more in my home for what had happened. But there was not much of anything.

We went on break soon after, and I'll never forget the day that we got back to school. Somebody said, "McKernan, you're not on the team anymore."

Now, you've got to recognize that when a team goes up, a team goes up. This is not like a provisional team. This is not a temporary team. This is the team. This is the team that's going to represent the school in the junior cup.

Somebody said, "Your name's not on the board."

I was shocked and absolutely floored, but I did what I always did. I put on a brave face and kind of laughed it off.

I remember walking up to the board. I made sure that I got there when no one was around. As I came up to the board, I had a different feeling. There wasn't the buzz of people. I don't remember what I smelled. I think I could just feel overwhelming, paralyzing fear. I got weaker and weaker and weaker as I got to the board. It's just all a blur.

All I remember is that my name was not on the board anymore.

That remains, to this day, the most humiliating time in my entire life: 650 people saw my name go up in lights, and 650 people knew my name was removed.

I was never told why. No one ever gave me the heads up that it was going to happen. I think I know the teacher who basically took my name off, but I never found out for sure.

It was just crushing. It brought me back to this place of, "Yeah, you're unworthy. You're not meant to be on things like that. You're not good enough to be on those types of teams."

It was very hard to deal with.

I know this sounds bad, and it was, but school wasn't all dark.

There was one teacher who believed in me. One teacher who saw something in me that I either could not see in myself or refused to see in myself.

His name was Trevor Garrett.

He was an extraordinary guy. We used to have both Honors

and Pass English. Honors is where the more advanced students would go, and the Pass classes were for the stupid kids, as some would say. And Trevor Garrett ran the Pass class.

I used to live for the days when I'd go to Trevor's class. He treated me like a human being. It's not like he did anything massively different to me than anyone else in his classes. But he saw something in me. He believed in me. He gave me this space. He made me feel that I was worthy. He honored my gifts and he didn't focus on my flaws.

And, as it turns out, I did have an ability to memorize things. For example, he would read a long story, like Horatio at the Bridge. And I could recite every single word. No other student could do that. I could memorize things that even he was surprised by.

Trust me, I was shocked, and he was surprised.

But the problem was, when it came to writing it down, I couldn't spell the words. Therefore, I was massively penalized in all the exams that I ever sat.

No matter what, Trevor continued to have this absolute belief in me. One person can be enough to keep hope alive.

A few years ago, we did our first documentary. I went to Dublin to do a showing in my home country. It's always very weird to go back to your own country, to the city you grew up in—Dublin—and to do a showing of a film that you feel proud about.

I remember being in the IFC in Dublin—the Irish Film Center, I think it's called—showing the film. I remember how, before I started, I did about a 15-minute bit of context, or conversation, just to set the film up.

For whatever reason, I realized one of the teachers that used to be in my school was there. I told the story about being in school, and how challenging it was, and I mentioned that one man in school believed in me, and his name was Trevor Garrett.

When you're standing at the front of a theater, there are a lot of lights on you, so you can't necessarily always recognize the faces in the room.

This person stood up, and all I could see was their shadow. As they walked down the steps toward the stage, and they came up, of course, lo and behold—it was Trevor Garrett!

He was looking a little bit older, like myself, but he had the same beautiful, smiley, accepting face that I always remembered as a kid.

He walked onto the stage, did not say a single word, put his arms around me, and held me. We embraced each other. He was holding me again, all these years later—this time, in a more physical sense than when I was in school. It was more of a spiritual sense at that time.

He didn't say one word, and he held me. The two of us shed a tear.

We finished our embrace, and he walked back, sat back down, and I looked around and said, "Okay, I'm done. We're going to just watch the movie now because I have nothing else to say. I'm a bit of a mess right now."

It was just a beautiful, circular time in my life. He's not the only one who had a huge impact on my life, but he was one of the very big people in my life. The big circle came back where he was in the audience. It was just a really, really proud moment for me.

Somebody asked me recently in a podcast interview, "What are you an expert in?" And I said, "Well, I don't really consider myself an expert in anything. But, if I had to, I would imagine that I'd consider myself an expert in misalignment."

What it feels like to be out of alignment. What it feels like to feel off in your identity, not understanding who you are. What it feels like to run from what you don't want, as opposed to moving toward what you do want.

I do believe—to my core—that our greatest gifts lie right next to our greatest pains.

I know that is true for me. I feel like my work has been crafted and inspired by the pain that I have experienced.

The reason I struggled for 37 years to find passion and purpose in this world is because I was unwilling to address and to lean into and to explore this pain—and therefore, the gift that sat right next door to it was left dormant.

I had to recognize and embrace the dark side of my experience. The pain and suffering of when I felt unseen or unheard, before I could walk into the light even a little. So I suppose the positive side of my story is that, to some extent, that's where the origin of One Last Talk was born.

I created One Last Talk because I know what it feels like to be unseen.

I know what it feels like to be unheard.

I know what it feels like to hold onto your truth and not share it.

I know what it feels like to feel pain.

To some extent, my journey and my pain are the very things that I want to help others through.

Of course, I can't do that for you. But I hope maybe I can help you, in some small way, do it for yourself.

If I look back and ask myself, "What is the most pivotal work I've ever done on myself?" it was uncovering and beginning to speak my truth.

The first time I went to therapy, I went begrudgingly. I thought, *Therapy is for other people. But for Philip McKernan? No fucking way.*

I remember walking into the room and seeing two seats. In one of the seats was a big box of Kleenex. I thought, *He must have a bad cold.* So, I sat in the other.

I was that naïve.

When he came in, he said, "That's my seat." All at once, I realized what the tissues were actually for.

I shouted at him, "You're not going to make me cry!"

We were about three and a half minutes in when the tears came. By the mid-point of the session, I was hoping there were more Kleenex in the cupboard.

At the end of the session, he said, "Okay, we're done now."

I said, "What do you mean we're done? I'm just getting started. Get me some more Kleenex, and let's get back at it."

I didn't realize how much anger, sadness, resentment, judgment, and shame I was carrying.

It was overwhelming. And quite scary, initially.

But as I moved through therapy, and as I uncovered and connected with my truth, I felt lighter and lighter. Eventually, I began to believe in myself. I thought, "*You know, McKernan, you're not a bad guy.*"

To make that realization—that I wasn't a bad guy at all—I had to acknowledge that my life was very painful at times. I had to face the reasons why I felt so bad about myself. I had to look at the shame and the judgment I felt from people.

I had to realize these emotions were in me. And once

I realized this, once I named these emotions, I felt so much lighter.

I wasn't fixed. I hadn't done all the work I would do eventually. But just the naming alone made such a big difference.

If I wanted to understand why I wished I could change my name, I had to dive into what made me feel so ashamed of myself to begin with.

Then, once I dove into all that pain, I had to figure out how to find purpose in my pain.

This was the hardest thing I ever had to do in my life. It tore me up, and it nearly broke me.

But I did it.

And now I'm determined to help people with similar pain to find their path to the other side.

That is the point of One Last Talk.

Even if you've gone through very different circumstances than I have, I want to show you how to face your pain, to stop your pain from trapping you. To instead get in touch with your truth and speak it, so

you can move past that pain—and potentially help others do the same.

I don't think I'm special. I believe, at the core, we all want to give back. We all want to make a difference.

The challenge for most people is how to actually go about doing that.

It seems difficult, but it's actually easy.

The problem is that we're often looking outside of ourselves for a way to give back.

I believe the source of giving should emanate from within. If we truly understand and connect with our truth—emotionally and not just intellectually—it actually shows us the answers.

I believe that once a person gets to the essence of who they are and really uncovers the truth they need to face and then speak, they will inevitably want to give back by helping others through the pain they've experienced.

So, while this might sound very simple—*that everyone wants to give back, and the best way they can give back is to connect with their pain and their truth and to speak it, and to thus help others experiencing that same pain*—it took me 44 years to understand.

You're about to read seven more One Last Talks. Each one is a real talk, given by a real person.

I start and finish each one with commentary to help you understand and contextualize them.

1.2

How One Last Talk Became Real: Bev

One Last Talk was initially born out of a frustration I had from being a speaker and working in the event space.

Frankly, I was tired of seeing speakers say one thing on stage, then get offstage and be somebody else. I was sick of the insincerity and inauthenticity.

I saw this multiple times, and I thought to myself, *Why not do something different? Why not get real people on stage and get them to open up in ways they never have so that people can relate?*

I wanted to create an environment where it was okay to share the darker stuff of life. Where regular people could say the types of things that were not being said on stages but needed to be heard.

I wasn't sure where this idea was going to go, if anywhere.

And then I met Bev.

When I met Bev, she was like a little flower that wouldn't allow herself to bloom. Yet, as I got to know her, I realized she had a massive heart. But she didn't see that. She didn't see her goodness. She didn't see how beautiful she really is and how she exudes goodness in the world.

I'll never forget the very first day in coaching, when I got Bev to stand up in front of the room with twelve other clients. I had her use a whiteboard to draw out what was going on in her life—just a quick sketch.

Her demeanor was like a young child who had been beaten her whole life. She looked at the floor and wouldn't look at anybody. I asked her to turn around and explain it, but she just couldn't. She had such shame that she felt like she didn't deserve to live. I had no idea why.

After a couple weekends together, I asked her, "What are you not telling us? What am I feeling that you're just not sharing?"

That's when she described finding her son after he committed suicide.

It explained everything.

Fast-forward about a year and a lot of pretty intense work with her. I sat down in front of the group of coaching clients that she was part of, and I shared the idea of One Last Talk.

I shared how I was sick and tired of inauthentic speakers on stage. I was sick of the lack of relatability from speakers to human beings in the audience.

I wanted to create the opposite.

My clients said, "Wow, it's an amazing idea. Who are the speakers?"

I said, "Real people. No big-name hotshots."

Again, they thought the idea sounded great—they were excited to see it. They wanted to know who the speakers would be.

I named each one of them in that room.

I was not prepared for what happened next. A couple of

them burst into tears. One person got angry. Another just didn't know what to do. One guy came over to hug me, but still said, "Oh shit, I don't want to do it."

The scene was so bizarre. None of them had seen it coming.

That was how One Last Talk was born. The idea triggered a lot of people emotionally, so of course I locked it in.

A few months later, I had that same group at a speaker retreat. I gave them one specific instruction: "Come with your One Last Talk."

When it was Bev's turn, she started talking about aboriginal First Nations injustices that happened in Canada. It was clear she was passionate about it. She felt guilty about it and wanted to do something about it.

This is a real and important issue. It matters to a lot of people.

But something was off. Bev is not part of the First Nations in any way. She doesn't even know them. The injustice these people suffered is real and should be talked about and be addressed. But she was not involved in it at all.

I stopped her, and asked, "Bev, is this really the One Last Talk you want to give? This is important, yes—but is this *the thing* that is most important to you, personally?"

She said it was, but I questioned her further. Finally, she said, "I don't know what else to talk about."

That's when the idea hit me: ***One Last Talk has to be your personal truth.***

It can't just be another talk about global warming, political problems, or aboriginal injustice. It has to be personal to you.

"Absolutely," she agreed, "but I don't know what to say."

What she was really saying was, "I don't have value. My truth doesn't matter."

I said, "What if you shared the story you shared with us last year, about your son?"

She was completely paralyzed by fear.

She didn't say it out loud, but I could tell she was thinking, *Why would I possibly share that story?*

I said, "You don't have to. It's your story. But I'm asking you to consider it."

Eventually, she decided to share her story.

BEV'S ONE LAST TALK

I'd been a single mom for about six years.

I had two sons—Greg, who was ten, and Timmy, who was seven—when I got my dream job. It was so awesome to me. I had a job with a lot of autonomy. I had a lot of creativity. I had growth opportunities. I had a bit of status. I had money. I got money.

I got lots of money.

So, for a single mom, that was awesome because it took the financial pressure off of having to raise kids and worrying about whether you'd be able to do it or not.

The next ten years were fabulous years. I had this great job. My kids were doing well. I met this awesome guy, David, and we got married. I had a handful of excellent friends that I had a lot of fun with. We did trips. It was just like—Jesus, this is the way life is meant to be lived.

It was great.

This one weekend, a bunch of us decided we would go out for dinner on a Friday night. I said, "Well, I'm going to get my hair done before I go to the dinner." Timmy, my 17-year-old at the time, heard me talking, and he said, "Hey. Any chance I could get a haircut while you're going?"

I said, "Well sure. You go there right after school, and I'll go right after work. You'll be done, and you can either wait for me to be done and we'll go home together, or you can walk home." It was just a ten-minute walk home. No worries.

So, I got over to the hairdresser's, and he's not there. I said, "So did he like his hair?"

She said, "He never showed up."

I said, "What? That's not cool. Did he call or anything?"

"No. No. I haven't seen hide nor hair of him."

So I got my hair done, and I went home, and I was annoyed. This is the emotion I had. Annoyance.

I was looking for him because I wanted to know why he stood

this lady up while she's trying to make a living. I looked around, and I said, "Dave, where's Timmy?"

He said, "I haven't seen him."

I said, "Well, he must be here, because I saw his shoes at the back door."

He said, "Oh. Well, he must have come in when I was doing something. I didn't see him. He didn't say hi or anything."

I went downstairs to his bedroom, and I knocked on the bedroom door and I said, "Timmy. I need to talk to you."

Nothing.

Nothing.

Then I tried the doorknob, and it was locked, so my annoyance escalated a little bit. I did the old coat hanger thing, and I opened the door.

There he was.

He was lying on his bed, and he was dead.

The 22 rifle that my husband had given him for Christmas was lying on the floor.

I have not understood the world since that moment.

I can't even describe it. Everything just stopped. The world stopped spinning.

It was so traumatic that it didn't settle in—like it wouldn't come into me for quite a while.

When it started to set in on me, it set in like this:

I felt like the most colossal failure that had ever walked this planet ever.

What kind of a mother has a kid that feels like…that wants to do that?

I just hated myself. I wanted to vomit myself out of myself.

Repulsion. Just disgust. I couldn't stand myself.

But you can't go through life like that. You have to somehow function.

I took all this disgusting stuff, these horrible feelings and this raw pain, and I put it in the closet, and I slammed the door, and I locked it, and I turned my back on it, and I walked away.

I put a mask on my face. Then I started going through my life, doing my thing. Keeping my job, still enjoying it, just not as much.

I went through 14 years of that. But there's a funny thing about closets. It doesn't matter what's in your closet. We all have a closet. Out from under the door, the shit seeps out, and the smell's there. It perverts you. It changes you, so you can't have an authentic relationship. You can't be real with anybody, because this is always interfering.

When you hate yourself that much, how can you possibly do anything that's worthwhile, because that's tainting everything?

I went through a long time of that, and I couldn't stand my friends that I used to love. They bugged me. Their kids were graduating. Their kids were doing shit, and my kid was moldering in the grave.

I fucking hated them.

Sorry.

I hated them sometimes.

There's another thing about family, and you probably all have had this experience. It's not cool to talk to other families about your pain. They can't tolerate it. They can't handle it either, and they don't want to know.

Everybody just assumed I'm okay, because I'm, you know, doing my thing. I'm out and about. But it's false.

It changed when I was with a handful of people and Phillip. That was the first time I turned back to the closet door and opened it. And it was so gross, and it was so scary, and I was so worried about what they were going to do.

They were going to just hate me as much as I do.

But they didn't. They didn't at all. They were quite the opposite. I'd never felt so supported and cared for. It was amazing to me.

The closet wasn't empty yet, but it was open at least. I didn't lock it after that.

Anyway, I've been working, and we've been clearing out the closet. Dave, my husband, passed away in the middle of this, because I couldn't deal with him. I just shut him out, and he's a guy that needed connection. He couldn't get it from me, so he went to cocaine and went to death.

I was sitting in my house one day. My eldest son, Greg, had moved out to start his life. Dave was gone. Tim was gone. And I'm sitting there with this bag of money that I had made off this fabulous job, because I was saving it for education and retirement.

I was looking at the bag of money thinking, "What is money?"

It doesn't come from nothing. It comes from moments of your life.

Every buck you pull out, that's a moment you throw out. You take a buck. You give.

It's a moment. It's a buck.

I looked at that, and I thought, "Oh. If I could have those moments back. Any of them, one of them, ten of them. I would take them in a heartbeat."

Anything I ever had, anything I will have, I would have given. But I can't have that, so I had to come to a different place.

The place I got to is that I first had to really appreciate and be grateful for the seventeen delicious years I had with that boy. I sit around and enjoy that a lot, myself. Then I have to thank him for this, because without him, I would have sat in front of my TV and had a small life doing small, petty things, worrying about the box.

He gave me this.

I'm not really fussy about him moving on, but I really am grateful for this. That I had the chance to grow and get past it and realize I do love myself. I'm not that despicable person that I thought I was.

I've never in my life witnessed anything like the silence after her talk.

One woman stood up from her seat in the middle of the room, walked onto the stage, and hugged Bev.

Even though I knew what was coming, tears still poured down my face. When I looked around the room, there wasn't a dry eye.

And this wasn't about being sad for the sake of being sad. Everyone was deeply moved by her and her story. She had trusted us and herself a tiny bit, just enough to get on stage and share the story in front of 150 people.

But if this talk was just about this horribly sad incident, then I doubt One Last Talk would exist. The world doesn't need more sad stories. What the world needs is people sharing their truths—sad or happy or depressing or painful—and then finding purpose in that pain to help others.

I had a list of questions I planned to ask Bev. I threw those out. I got on stage and asked the audience one question:

"What are you going to do because of this talk? What are you going to do differently in your life?"

Every hand in the house went up. I got answers like:

"I'm going to take my daughter on date night every week."

"I'm going to lock my phone up when I am home with my kids."

"I'm going to stop worrying about money and start spending time with my kids."

"I'm going to hug my kids every morning and spend time with them talking about their day."

It went on and on.

The purpose of the talk was not just Bev telling her story. Yes, that was crucial, but what made it so impactful was what happened after. How she used her story to help other people see things in their lives.

If you are reading this and thinking, *I can't even imagine that*, then try the same exercise. Ask yourself: What are you going to do differently because of this story?

Because I will tell you what I told that audience:

You don't need to lose your children to wake up as a parent.

The Power of Transparency: Brian

One day, I was chatting with Brian, and he said, "I love the concept of One Last Talk."

I said, "If I asked you to do one, what would you speak about?"

Immediately, Brian responded, "The Five Fs."

He used the Five Fs as a framework for focusing on what matters: faith, family, finances...stuff like that.

I rolled my eyes.

Sure, the Five Fs are interesting. But he didn't understand

what One Last Talk is all about. So, I patiently explained it to him.

I wasn't sure if he got it, because he looked away. But then looked back at me, and his eyes had completely changed.

They held a single, pure emotion: paralyzing fear.

"I know exactly what I would talk about."

In that moment, I loved him. Before I even heard what the topic was, I said, "You're in."

I didn't even ask him more questions. I could feel it. I just knew.

The process I use to select who will speak at the One Last Talk events is pretty intuitive. I'm always looking for people who I believe are willing to be really open about their truths.

For the event, every speaker gets to invite one family member. It cannot be a cousin or colleague. It must be an immediate family member. Brian brought his dad, who's a pastor.

When it was Brian's turn to go, he put it all out there.

BRIAN'S ONE LAST TALK

I'm going to share with you my journey.

As Philip said, I had another idea for a talk, but Philip has a gift for asking powerful questions. He stopped me in my tracks, and said, "Brian, I have two young children. If you could leave them one gift, would it really be the Five Fs?"

It was one of those tunnel vision moments, where I knew what I needed to do.

What I want to talk to you about is self-love and forgiveness.

I grew up in a very loving environment in North Jersey just outside of Manhattan—wonderful loving parents, a brother and sister, great family and friends.

I didn't have really much to complain about, but something happened when I got to the age of about 12 or 13. My hormones started going, and I got into an incredible amount of shit.

I can make you guys feel better. Who here has skeletons in the closet, or something that maybe you may have done in the past that you're not proud of?

Well, I'm going to make you feel better, because I'm going to outdo you with the shit that I got into.

At 13, I lost my virginity and started sleeping with as many women as possible. I started smoking pot. I started drinking heavily. I started getting arrested. Between the years of 13 and 21, I probably got arrested a dozen times. All kinds of crazy shit. The details are not important.

Fast-forward to 21 years old. I went out to Tempe, Arizona, to be with some friends. What I did there, with my college degree, is started to sell pot for a living. So I put my college degree to great use.

We moved a lot of marijuana from across the border of Mexico into Arizona, and then dispersed it out through North America. That's how I used my college degree.

My college degree—I didn't even think about this before—but my college degree was in criminal justice, so what's the irony in that?

It's very hot here in the summer. I decided to go to Yellowstone National Park. I went with a girl I'd only known for three weeks, but she trusted me enough to jump in my car with me and, I think, four or five pounds of pot in the trunk.

Three weeks into that summer season, she moved on from me. I met another young lady—she was actually one of my best customers. She bought a lot of pot from me, and she went back to Phoenix with me.

Just to reiterate: I moved up with one woman and four or five pounds of pot, and then moved back with another woman a couple months later, with very little pot because we had smoked it all.

I get back to Phoenix with this young lady, and it's a very tumultuous, passionate relationship that lasted three months. Very unhealthy, a lot of fighting—not physical fighting, nothing like that. But it just didn't work out. She said, "I'm out of here. I'm going back to Chicago."

I got a call two months later from her. She was pregnant with my child. I don't know if anyone has gotten a call like that from someone that you don't love and you're disconnected from, but it's the worst fucking call you can ever get.

I went into a tailspin. I was already numb, as some of the other speakers have said. Depressed, basically just walking through life stoned. To get a call like that, it was a slap in the face.

She told me she wanted to have an abortion. That's the route that we went.

That was a very, very difficult thing for me to swallow. I was raised in a Catholic environment, so this is the cardinal sin.

I hated myself. I became depressed, self-loathing, just wanted to crawl up in a corner. I guess I was completely numb, but I still didn't change my lifestyle. I continued to date around.

Fast-forward three months. I got a call from another young lady I'd hooked up with a few times: "Brian, I'm pregnant with your child."

At that point in my life, I was so numb. I don't even know how to describe it. We went back and forth by phone. She came down to Phoenix and decided that she wanted to get an abortion as well.

Now, within six months of my life, I've been arrested, have impregnated two young ladies, and have gone through two abortions.

It was a very, very deep, dark place in my life.

I decided I had to get the hell out of Arizona. I thought my phones were tapped. I was paranoid about cops kicking in the door and arresting me. And after going through those experiences with those women, Arizona and me weren't getting along very well.

I decided to move to Santa Barbara, California. I was broke when I moved there, but I didn't continue to sell pot. I woke up a little bit—enough to stop the lifestyle. I was going to try to earn some money legitimately.

I waited tables and bussed tables and shoveled horse shit at a horse ranch north of Santa Barbara for my first legitimate jobs out of college.

I was very depressed. I went to a shrink in downtown Santa Barbara—a beautiful young lady who had just graduated from UCSB with a psych degree. I was probably one of her first patients. Maybe her first patient.

I spilled my guts to her—everything I just told you, but with a lot more detail. I saw her weekly for about a year. The takeaway was trying to find self-love and forgiveness through the chaos that I'd created.

She said, "Brian, find your favorite picture of yourself as a baby. Find that picture, laminate it, put it in your wallet, and when you feel like shit and when all these emotions arise or you're having a shitty day, take out the picture. Look into the eyes of yourself as a child, and everything will dissipate."

She was right.

About three-quarters through that year, I came to one of our sessions, and she said, "Brian, I've got to tell you something. I'm pregnant."

No, it's not my child. It's not a third one. She's a beautiful young lady with a loving husband, starting her family.

"I've decided to close down my practice. I want to be a full-time mother."

Totally stoked for her, but a little bit scared because she was sort of my shoulder to cry on. I floundered around in Santa Barbara for another year. I started surfing. I started spending a lot of time in mother nature.

One day the surf was flat, so I decided to go up the hill to go for a hike. I came back down the trail and my car was parked in a place called Mount Calvary, which is a retreat for young priests who are in training. I saw this guy walking across the parking lot, and I said, "Can I chat with you?"

It was totally impromptu. I didn't even know him or know I was going to cross his path, but I just wanted to spill my beans. I was carrying these abortions around with the weight of the world on my shoulders.

Went in, sat down with him, spilled my beans...and I remember there being a really uncomfortable moment of silence in the room. It's, again, one of those tunnel vision moments.

He said, "Brian, there are two ways that you can process this. You can continue to beat yourself up over it, which you and I know is not working, or you can realize that you now have a gift of two guardian angels that are going to carry you around and protect you for the rest of your life."

The weight of the world lifted off my chest that day.

Everyone goes through shit. Life is a process, not an event, and self-love and self-forgiveness are each a process, not an event. You've got to get up every day and do it.

We think that we're human beings, and once in a while we get lucky and have a spiritual experience. I disagree.

We are perfect, loving, divine, spiritual beings trying to figure out how to move around in these meat bags that we've been gifted with temporarily. Not the other way around. I think that is the quantum leap in moving toward self-love and forgiveness.

Thank you.

He had never shared this full story with anybody, ever, aside from his wife.

After his talk, I joined Brian on stage. His dad was sitting to our right. I could see the fear still in Brian's eyes, like he had been dreading this his whole talk.

I said, "First of all, thank you for sharing. I don't know if it's appropriate, and I apologize in advance if it's not, but I just want to acknowledge Brian's father. I just want to acknowledge that you are in the room and that this must be really difficult."

I was about to go into another question when, out of the corner of my eye, I saw his hand go up.

"Can I say something?"

I had no idea where this was going. He could have said anything.

The mic made its way over to him, and he started to speak.

"I just want to tell you..."

This is all he got out before he started bawling. He kept crying and said:

"Son, all I can tell you is that when I look at you with your children, I'm just beyond proud of the father and human that you've become. And I love you unconditionally."

Brian completely broke down. Those were the words he so desperately wanted to hear his whole life.

It's Not Just about You: Quan

One time, I was invited to give a speech in Downtown Vancouver. Afterward, this guy walked up to me and introduced himself. He said, "I want to do what you do. Will you teach me how?"

I asked this guy what he meant.

He said, "I want to inspire people."

"Great," I said. "How?"

"Well, through speeches and different kinds of speaking," he responded.

I challenged him: "Great. Why not do it right now?"

"I knew you were going to ask me that," he said. Then he gives me his whole story. "I was working and very successful. I had a lot of money, but I lost it all through gambling and drugs. So now I'm kind of building myself back up again. Once I'm successful again, then I'll be ready to do it."

"Great. But I ask again, why not do it right now?"

"I don't think I'm ready."

"Sounds like you're looking for the perfect story."

"Well, you know..."

He hesitated, and the conversation stalled. In other words, he was saying yes, that was exactly what he was doing.

I put my arm around him and took him over to the window. I said:

"You see down there? There are gamblers down there. Drug addicts. People who don't even know yet they will be gamblers or drug addicts. People recovering and just on the verge of moving back into that darkness. And you're sitting here waiting for the perfect story. Until you make this fully about them, you have no right to be a speaker."

It was harsh, but I had to tell him the truth.

He was absolutely pushed back. He couldn't believe I responded the way I did. He was expecting me to say, "Oh, keep at it. Don't worry. When you've built up a story backlog, then you can go for it. Do it when the time is right."

Fuck that.

I said, "You're talking about where your story is now. It contains you, but it doesn't have to be about you. It *does* have to affect other people. You can go beyond your story itself, and you can dig into your truth, and you can share it to help others. Right now. Today."

I use the phrase "your pain has a purpose" over and over again. This is what I'm getting at. Yes, you need courage to speak what you're afraid of, but you have to have *context* for that courage.

With One Last Talk, people often don't realize until afterward that their pain has purpose for others. I try to help people understand that idea in advance, because that provides great motivation and an invitation for the speaker.

In fact, I will often go so far as to tell people that their pain happened for a reason.

Some people get pissed off by that statement. It's hard to think you were raped for a reason, abused for a reason, or depressed for a reason.

That's not what I'm saying. I'm not saying people deserved what happened, or it was fated, or they created it themselves, or anything like that.

What I'm saying is that they can't run from it and pretend it didn't happen. They have to accept it and then deal with it. And the next iteration of that acceptance of pain is to share it.

What I am ultimately saying is that you can use your pain for a purpose.

And I am also saying that sharing becomes very therapeutic for the person sharing and allows them to forgive themselves while still helping other people.

Quan's One Last Talk was a great example of this.

When I first met Quan, I was sitting next to him at an event. I could feel his awkwardness.

We were just chatting, and I could feel his anxiety. I knew they had former convicts at this event, so I just made an assumption. I felt that I needed to say this to him:

"I don't know you well, but you belong in this room."

That made him tear up. I could sense his feeling of not belonging, and his awkwardness, and his shame, and so on and so forth. I think I connected with him in this way because I also struggle deeply with these same issues.

I knew that Quan had a story that, if he shared it, would not only help him, but it would help all of us.

QUAN'S ONE LAST TALK

On January 15th, 1999, I shot and killed Mr. Minh Nguyen.

I also tried to shoot and kill his three friends, David Tran, Vincent Vivathanakul, and Andrew Vivathanakul.

I was tried for the death penalty, but because I lied at trial, I got rid of evidence, and I coached witnesses, I was only found guilty of second degree murder and sentenced to 15 years to life in the California prison system.

But I wasn't born a murderer.

I was born in Vietnam and settled here in the United States as a toddler. We lived in Provo, Utah—and Utah, for me, was a beautiful place for my childhood, for the most part.

I did experience what I've come now to understand as racism. One of the earliest experiences I remember that left a big imprint on me was when my younger brother and I were playing with our GI Joes in the ditch. I was about eight years old, and some older kids were on the other side of the fence. They told us, "Get out of here. Go back to your country. Go home," and called us some racial words.

The fence looked so big. I didn't think they would be able to get over it. So, we told them to make us get out of there.

Those kids jumped the fence pretty quickly and started chasing us. They had some adults there, too. I think they may have been their uncles or perhaps their father, or something. Or older brothers. But I had dropped some of my action figures and my younger brother stopped to pick them up. I remember the older kids caught up, pushed my brother on the ground, and put dirt in his mouth. I stood there crying.

I went home crying, and my father, when he found out what happened, he said, "You never, ever let anybody harm your family."

I felt so ashamed, and I remember telling myself, "I'm not going to let anybody harm my family ever again."

My father was diagnosed with leukemia later that year. We moved here. We moved out to California, and he passed away when I was 13. I remember I was so angry at my mom, my dad, God, the world—but I found a lot of acceptance in the criminal and gang lifestyle.

By the age of 17, I was arrested for the first time, and I went down a long, dark path that ultimately culminated in the murder of another human being.

I'm also ashamed to say that, for the first 11 years of my prison sentence, I felt no sense of remorse. I'd never grasped the finality of what I did until I started asking myself those questions:

"What am I doing here? Am I meant to die in prison? Is this it for me?"

I remember finding solace reading books about the saints, and I realized every single one of these human beings were very flawed at one time or another. Yet they were able to leave such legacies and were able to touch so many lives.

I remember asking myself, "Why could I not do the same thing in here?" Even if I am to die in prison, why could I not leave some type of legacy?

I remember the morning when it shifted in my head that I had a choice in this.

I was on the prison yard. My head was filled with the teachings of the saints, and somewhere in my mind, it just clicked. Like, "I can make a choice. I can leave a legacy. I can become a better person."

I remember distinctly, I was standing by the fence. I felt the warmth of the sun. I saw the dew on the individual blades of grass. For the first time, probably in 12 years, I heard a sparrow that was sitting in the razor wire, chirping.

And suddenly, prison was no longer this ugly, harsh place. It took on such a soft light for me. From that day forth, I began connecting with other human beings, even while in prison—even while doing my life sentence.

I remember one of the first NPR radio interviews they did with me after release. The reporters were asking about the groups that I had created with some of the other men that were inside, and somewhere in the process of the interview, she asked me, "What are you in prison for?"

I said, "Murder."

I remember everything in me wanting to explain, because everything in me up to that point had always explained: wait, but it was a gang crime. But, wait, it was this. Or wait...

But I just sat with it, and I was totally terrified of what she was thinking of me.

The longer I sat with it, the more I felt, like, liberated in a sense. Like, "Yes, I did do that, but yes, I'm no longer that person."

From that day forth, when it was ever brought up, I just said I was in prison for the murder of another human being.

I remember one of the most difficult conversations I've ever had to have was with my mother. This was in 2015, right before I went to my board hearing, and she was very concerned about what was going to happen at the board hearing—if they were going to let me go or if they were going to deny me.

And I said, "Mom, it doesn't matter. Let's just be happy that I'm alive. Let's be happy that you get to hug and kiss me."

She said, "Yes, but I want you to go home."

I said, "But Mom, you do realize why I'm in prison, right? Let's be grateful that you can hug and kiss me. There's another mother just like you who doesn't have a son that's alive because of what I did."

I've been home now about two years. I was paroled. Governor Brown signed my paperwork after the parole hearing, and they let me go home. Now I get to spend so much time with my mom, and I love it. Every Sunday, we'll go to Mass, and then after that, we'll have our Sunday lunch date. We get to eat lunch together, and I love it.

We sit across from each other, and I can just feel the joy oozing out of her, because that's how I feel with it. We're actually sitting at a table instead of a small prison table. We're eating good food instead of vending machine food.

But there's still something that weighs heavy on me. Back in 2011, when I started to grasp what remorse was, I wrote a letter to the mother of the man I killed and I sent it off to the Office of Victim Services.

I remember when I first wrote the letter, it was like three, four pages long, all these eloquent-sounding words. I realized I was hiding. I was using those words to hide behind it, and I thought to myself, "What can I really say to the mother of the man that I killed?"

If I had been killed that night, what could somebody say to my mom to alleviate her pain? And I realized there was nothing, so I cut down my letter. I chopped it down to about six, seven sentences, and I sent it off.

A couple months later, the Office of Victim Services sent the original letter back to my central file, which meant that she never received it, because she never registered with the Office of Victim Services. My friends on the yard with me told me they were very happy that I got the letter back, because it meant she wasn't going to show up to my parole hearing.

But I wanted her to receive that letter. Part of me felt guilty, because then I realized this increased my very slight chances of parole. But then I felt guilty because I wanted to go home with my mom.

So, I still have that letter, and I wanted to read it today because she never received it. It's dated November 5, 2011.

"Dear Mrs. Julie Nguyen,

I want you to know I am truly sorry for taking your son's life. I am sorry for forever tainting the way you may see the world and taking the joy out of it.

I pray that in some small way, my words could provide some measure of healing for you. I want you to know that I am not the same person that committed this violent and senseless act, and I'm living a life from here on out to honor the man who I will be forever paying my penance for, your son, Minh Nguyen."

Thank you.

That speech was incredibly moving, and an amazing thing happened afterwards.

First, a friend of mine who was in the audience, Derek, stood up and asked to speak. Derek is a serious guy, very successful, and doesn't mince words:

I feel like I owe Quan an apology.

When we met at MasterMind Talks this year, Quan was there with a few others from his organization for ex-convicts. And I sort of felt at the time, without having any animosity toward him at all, that it would be safer and easier to talk to some of the other individuals. The ones who hadn't murdered anybody.

I like to view myself as a fairly non-judgmental person... but I absolutely judged him. And I think in hearing his story, I recognize what I did.

And it made me realize that it's something that I need to look at a little bit more closely. In order for him to live out his life, he needs more people to not judge him, not to take perception as reality, and just sort of be able to receive him a little bit more openly.

So, I'm going to work on that, in all areas of my life, and with regard to Quan.

I have to admit, I struggled with the same thing Derek did.

Before I asked Quan to speak, I was concerned what people would think of me putting him on the stage. I was thinking, "Oh my God. I have to put him on stage. What will people think? What will they say about the YouTube video?" I was concerned that people would judge us and that they wouldn't accept him in the room.

And then I got mad at myself for being so concerned about what other people thought. As a result, I ended up becoming quite protective around him. Especially because I know him, I know what a beautiful soul he has, and how hard he has worked to honor the life he took and become a good man.

The second thing was just as remarkable (at least to me):

My kids—Charlie, who's nine, and Maggie, who's six—were at this One Last Talk event. My kids don't hug you. If you came to our house and said, "Hey Maggie, give me hug," it's not happening. Even if you give her candies and you buy her drawings, she still won't give you hugs.

They both went up to Quan after the speech. I did not ask them to. I did not even mention this. They both went up and hugged Quan and said, "We really liked your talk."

Quan just stood there, tearing up as my kids held him. It was beautiful.

1.5

You Have a Truth to Share That Matters: Donna

I get this question about One Last Talk often:

"Will people care about my truth?"

The simple answer is yes.

So many people struggle seeing the value in their own truth. This is true for me and my family. I think of my wife, Pauline, remembering her little pink baby stroller. She had tears rolling down her face, and I asked her what had happened.

She said that when she was three, her family left Scotland to return to Ireland. They didn't have much money, so her doll and baby stroller were everything to her. But they left the baby stroller for her doll behind. They remembered everything except Pauline's prized possession.

Telling the story 40 years later, she was embarrassed and berated herself. Still, she couldn't help how she felt—how sad it made her.

"How could they possibly forget one of the two most sacred things in my life?" she said.

I asked her what she thought it all meant.

She said she hadn't thought about that before.

Finally, she said, "I suppose I felt that because the stroller didn't matter, I didn't matter."

How could a stroller have such repercussions for a grown woman? Pauline felt so stupid crying over a baby stroller.

But just because others might have stories that are more "dramatic" or "important" doesn't mean the stroller is not significant.

The pain is the same.

That statement really pisses some people off, but it's true.

The pain is exactly the same.

It's not about the circumstances being more or less significant; it's about the subjective pain that you feel.

So yes—your truth IS significant. And YES, you should speak it. And yes, others WILL care about it.

You've got to remember, by sharing your pain and your truth, you are not only helping yourself, *you are helping everyone who hears it as well.*

I'm not suggesting that you walk up to a stranger on the street and tell them your truth. That person might judge the shit out of you.

One Last Talk is about sharing your truth in an environment that is safe and non-judgmental for the speaker and the listener.

By connecting with your darkest story, then sharing it— letting out your pain, expressing what you're most deeply ashamed about—you free yourself at a core level.

But you also realize you don't get rid of the truth. You can't do that. Getting rid of it should never be the goal.

Instead, you begin to notice other people who are sharing

in your pain. You think, "Oh my God, we have the exact same shame."

Now you start to see that your pain can help others. And you realize that your pain has purpose. Not just for you, but for others.

At every turn, I remind people: it's not about you. It's not about you. It's not about you.

The reality is that someone's emotional involvement in your One Last Talk is held by the glue of empathy and nothing more. And empathy is nothing more than their ability to project themselves into your shoes.

If someone is empathetic toward you, it means that deep within themselves, they recognize a certain shared humanity. As soon as a similarity from your story and theirs strikes a chord, they will suddenly and instinctively want you to achieve whatever it is that you desire, and they will begin rooting for you.

When they identify with you and your desires in life, they are in fact rooting for their own desires in life. It has nothing to do with compassion or altruism. People empathize for very personal, if not egocentric, reasons.

The gift of your story gives them an opportunity to temporarily live a life beyond their own, to desire and struggle in a world and time different than their own, and to be inspired and learn from a life and story other than their own.

Basically, by sharing your truth—*no matter how insignificant you think it is*—you not only help yourself, you also help them.

The best example of this is Donna. Donna is a very conservative, proper woman, but she has a boldness in her that she never gives herself permission to express.

When I first started meeting with Donna, I noticed she still wore her wedding ring, even though she was separated from her husband. She wouldn't allow herself to admit the reality to herself or to her daughters. The divorce had gone through legally, but it was a big point of shame for her.

In coaching, we got her to the point where she accepted that the relationship was over. She literally removed her ring, which was very symbolic of her reality setting in.

Then she had a conversation with her daughters, which she had worried about. She sat them down and told them that she and their dad were not together anymore.

They said, "Jeez, we thought you had cancer or something. We already knew that."

The only person who was still holding onto the lie was Donna.

When I reached out to Donna and asked her to do her One Last Talk, she was shocked by the invitation. She was in that place of thinking, "I don't know what I'd share. Are you sure you want me?"

She said the last thing she'd ever want to talk about publicly was her divorce.

But she ended up getting on stage and sharing the story of her dysfunctional, abusive relationship and how she found the courage to leave.

DONNA'S ONE LAST TALK

When Philip asked me to speak, I was one of those people who said, "Well, what would I possibly have to share?"

I thought hard, and with the spirit of the event in mind, I decided to share the most difficult thing I've been through: my divorce.

I had to think about how to relay it today, and I was very tempted to go with Five Easy Steps to Divorce; but somehow, I don't think that's what you guys are here for. So, I'll share the real story.

Before I get started, though, the lawyer in me says I must start with a disclaimer. Something like, "This is for general purposes only. It is only the interpretation of the presenter and may not be suitable for all audiences."

Kidding aside, I must say that I'm not a proponent of divorce. When I married, I married for life.

But there we were, 20-plus years into our marriage and very unhappy. Our relationship had worsened, and we were both miserable. Even worse, the kids were being caught up in our verbal fighting and passive-aggressive behaviors.

Ultimately, I could see that the marriage was not repairable. Over those years, I felt a heavy burden of stress, living in that relationship, in that circumstance. I often thought my head would burst, and sometimes I even thought it might kill me.

Deep down, we still loved each other, but the problem of alcoholism runs deeper than that, and it still hurts to think that my husband chose the bottle over his wife and family—a wife and family that he loved from the bottom of his heart, as he would say.

There I was, living a lie, pretending everything was fine with my family and friends, living with the guilt and shame of that lie. I was sad but feeling powerless to help that the kids were getting caught up in our fighting and being hurt by it. I was exhausted from the games and the disrespect, but I was worried about telling my family, especially my grandma. Should I wait and spare her the news? She was 90, after all.

These are the things that went through my head.

As bad as the situation was, we were a family. We were supposed to be together. If we split, what then?

I had visions of the pain it would cause the kids, being from a broken home.

I was ashamed that somehow, I had allowed the marriage to fail, and I was scared about being divorced.

I thought that, if we split, I would carry that with me forever.

On top of that, I had fears of dealing with the custody of the children, selling the family home, splitting the assets, so much stuff…I had so much fear.

About that time, I was in an event with Philip. That weekend, it became clear to me that, even though life for the kids and myself would be horrible as far as I knew, staying was worse. Every day I stayed in that relationship, disrespecting myself, it was hurting me more and it was hurting the kids.

That day, I made the decision in my heart that it was time to move forward, but my mind didn't know the Five Easy Steps. Off I went to the bookstore, because I do believe that all answers can be found at the bookstore. I grabbed a few books and sat in the corner. I didn't want to go home. I just sat there reading, sitting with my new decision, and feeling a huge weight off my shoulders.

I did purchase a couple books, but it was really just to get my mind in alignment with my gut.

I told my husband. I said, "It's over." After all the fighting we had done, he knew it was over, too.

The most difficult part was sharing it with the kids. I thought we should tell the kids together, but my husband wouldn't have any part of it, and I was terrified.

One of my daughter's friends' family had split, and that girl had missed school for weeks and was sobbing. I didn't want to bring that onto my own kids.

I avoided telling the kids, and I stressed myself out for months.

Finally, I found a time where they had nothing going on for

the rest of that afternoon or the next day, for good measure, and said, "We need to have a conversation."

As soon as we gathered together, I started talking and sobbing and spitting out the words. I looked at them, and they were chuckling.

After all my stress, they said they already knew.

The big magic was now it was out in the open, and they were able to ask questions that concerned them. That conversation was a short one, but the door was opened—not that it was easy for the kids.

Probably one of the worst moments, though, was moving day. I had to be the strong, responsible one, as usual. My husband didn't even come to help. He didn't sort his things. He didn't pack his things. He sent a friend and a huge roll-off garbage bin.

It was so sad for me to see our things being thrown away. Everything was happening too quickly for me to manage. Things that I had set aside to keep were disappearing.

I felt that represented—at that moment—my marriage and my life going into the garbage can. I felt like my heart was being ripped out of my chest that day.

A couple years later, I was meeting with my friend and realtor, and he commented on how well I had handled the move. I confessed that, when no one was looking, I was bawling my eyes out.

From there, I bought a big house on the hill because I was still holding onto image, and I felt it was my responsibility to continue to provide a nice home for my kids. Unfortunately, even though I was already working, I had to get another job to pay for that nice home. I found myself working full time in the day, and then in the evenings I was working on my own business. It began to wear me down after a while.

Reflecting, I did it to keep up appearances. I did it for my own ego, and I did it because it was what I thought I needed to do to take care of others. Being the responsible one.

After a couple years of that, I decided—enough. I needed to make a change. I quit my job, left my accounting profession behind, and decided to take a year off and go back to school for holistic nutrition. It's something I had wanted to do for a while, but I had never thought about taking some time out and putting myself first.

It started with quitting my job, and the next thing you know, I was selling my house and moving to Vancouver as well. Really, it started with putting myself and my happiness first.

I absolutely loved school. I loved the curriculum, I loved the teachers, I loved my classmates, and I absolutely loved living in Vancouver.

At some point after the separation, I took the time out—I took the opportunity—to apologize to my girls. The last years of marriage had been difficult, and I apologized to them for the backlash and the mean things that I had said and done in the midst of the fighting with my husband.

Having that conversation has brought us closer together than before. We're able to laugh at some of our indiscretions, and we've been able to set aside judgment for compassion, acceptance, and support. For that, I'm extremely grateful.

Looking back, I was paralyzed about going down the road of divorce, because I didn't know where it would lead me. I can tell you, it is pretty much impossible to know—good or bad.

These things weren't on my radar or even potentially comprehensible, but I know that if I can follow and stay on the path to my happiness, good things can happen.

I could never have comprehended that, five years ago when I started the separation, I would be here, living in Vancouver as a holistic nutritionist, working reasonable hours and absolutely loving life.

A few months ago, I was wandering down Main Street with one of my daughters. We were in a shop, and she looked up on the wall, and she said, "That's you."

I looked up and there was a banner. It said, "Living the Dream."

It took me a little bit. I realized, whoa, that IS me.

Over the years, I tried very hard to be a good role model for my two daughters. I didn't hold up to it for a little bit there; but in finding the strength to leave my marriage and stand up for myself, I believe that I'm sending my girls a strong message that they are important, they deserve respect, and they need to follow their own happiness. They seem to be. They are both living their absolutely unique and wonderful lives, and I'm so proud of them. I think they are living the dream.

One last thing. Last month, I was asked out on a date. For the first time in five years, I found myself skipping and dancing around the house, and skipping down the road if I thought no one was looking.

At the same time, I was terrified, and I thought, why go? It'll never work out. It's pointless. Just stay at home and be safe.

In between those thoughts, I cried a few tears of joy.

My heart is coming back to life.

One of Donna's daughters was in the back of the room when her mother gave her talk. This is what happened after the speech:

Philip: *Donna's daughter is in this room. I don't know what I'm asking her. Speak, share? I did get her permission a few minutes ago. She said, "What question are you going to ask me?" And I couldn't come up with one, for obvious reasons.*

Can I ask you to stand as well, please?

I just wonder what it's like to be in a house where your mother is courageous enough to make these really big decisions. What kind of an impact does that make on you as you look at your life unfolding in the future?

Donna's Daughter: *I think it makes the biggest difference. I think that if I look at how I saw my future when I was younger, when we were living in our old family home, when she was with my father. It was just all very typical, you know. They were both doing things that they didn't like.*

None of us were really happy, but we were just playing all of that out.

So, I thought to myself, "Okay, in my future, I'll go to school for something that maybe I don't really want to do because I'm good at it, and I'll make lots of money because I was told that that was really important, and I should start thinking about that."

That's what I thought for a while, but then my mom started making all of these crazy choices.

She talked a lot in her speech about being so worried about us being from a broken home, and I never—I never would have put that word to myself or to the situation at all.

If I look at her now and the choices that she made—even just moving out of the town we were in to Vancouver—that opened so many doors for me. Maybe it's something that I wouldn't have done myself, but she brought me there.

And now I have so many more opportunities, and I feel

like what I'm doing right now with my life—I'm so happy. And it's nothing that I would've ever imagined, because I didn't go to college. I didn't do all of this stuff that I really was set on.

I thought that that was the path. But then she started branching off, and I was like, "Oh, maybe it's okay for me to do what I actually want to do. Maybe I can take these risks, even if maybe that's not a good paying job. Maybe I don't know where that's going to lead me 20 years in the future."

But maybe that's okay, because she's okay. So that's something.

Philip: *That's a lot more than something. Thank you. Remember: it's not about you. It's not about you.*

If you want inspiration—if you want some motivation, if you want to hold onto something that's bigger than you, and you want something to help you make the changes that you often don't want to make on your own—stop making the journey about you.

Consider the impact that you're going to make on somebody else close to you or around you.

When you change your world, everybody else's worlds change as well.

Donna, thank you so much.

Also, I want to point something out: Donna's story was profoundly impactful to people, but it wasn't a dramatic story. It was fairly simple.

And because of this—because it wasn't dramatic with a big reveal—she was so concerned about sharing it.

She got past this by understanding that the key point of giving a One Last Talk is not whether or not your truth has the capacity to affect others.

It's imperative that you share your truth, no matter what.

If you don't share it, you'll continue to suffer, even in ways you do not fully understand.

So many people struggle with this. The problem is that so many people don't want the world to know who they really are. Part of them says, "I want to find my passion and live a purposeful life." The other part says, "I don't even want to see *myself*—forget letting the world see me."

There are many reasons why people think they shouldn't share their truths or let the world see them.

One reason is because most people are never told that

this is something they could do. In fact, they are told the opposite.

When you're sent to school (and this applies around the globe), you're told what to do. You're told what's important and what to learn. When I walked down the corridor of my school, there was never a classroom that said, "Hey, come in and get to know who you are." It's always, "Hey, here's geography," or, "Here's algebra." There is no class that represents the rest of our lives.

Even our parents are often too busy telling us what to do and what not to do and who to be in society.

But almost no one helps us to make time for our truth.

When do we ever stop—as a child or an adult—and connect with who we really are at our emotional core? With our truth?

The result is that so many people struggle with purpose and meaning. We don't put value on our own personal narratives.

When somebody is an expert on a subject like accounting, they're willing to talk about what they know. But when I ask that same accounting expert to share part of their personal truth, they express a lot of self-judgment toward it.

On the one hand, some people feel their truth won't be interesting. On the other, some are afraid they'll come across like they're bragging. They're more familiar with having heroes on this kind of pedestal, so they can comfortably say, "I'm not as good as you. I'm not enough."

I think One Last Talk helps you solve this problem. It challenges you to get in touch with what is really important—the essence of your truth.

You think by running from it, by putting it in a box and burying it six feet under the ground, that it's dealt with. It's not. Sooner or later, you'll realize that it still pulls very deep emotional strings and is affecting you on a fundamental level.

You have to get to the darker part and shine a light on it. It's like going into the darkness of your soul but giving yourself permission to turn the light on once you get there.

When you're encouraged to get in touch with it and share it publicly, to bring it out into the world, it's like breathing from your stomach instead of the top of your chest for the first time. The oxygen down there is stale, and you've literally just let it out for the first time in your life.

This is because sharing is the last stage of processing when it comes to emotional pain.

The challenge is to show people your own individual truth, through your own lens.

There's no advice in that. That's vulnerability.

My definition of vulnerability is very simple: *vulnerability equals truth*.

When you share your truth, when you are truly vulnerable, people won't just accept you. They'll literally fall in love with you in that moment because they've connected with you so deeply. Because sharing your truth and being vulnerable allows them to see themselves, which is such a rare and precious gift.

Everyone Can Relate: Rob Friend

The listener actually gets more than they might expect from seeing a One Last Talk.

Take, for example, Rob Friend. Rob is a former professional soccer player who spoke about playing in front of 70,000 people and scoring the winning goal. He got promoted to Bundesliga, which is one of the great soccer leagues in the world.

He began his talk by saying how he would sit in the dressing room, put on his jersey, and listen to "Don't Stop Believing" by Journey.

During his talk, I played that music for him.

ROB FRIEND'S ONE LAST TALK

A few weeks ago, I was asked to speak at this event, and I thought, "Yeah, I've played soccer in front of 70,000 people. How hard can this be?"

But I want to puke right now.

That song that was playing before—that was my pregame song. "Don't Stop Believing." Funny enough, Phillip asked me a few weeks ago what the song was that I listened to before games, and that was that. Now I know why he did.

He pumped me up a little bit. I think I was stretching in the corner there. I was ready for the game. Told my wife this morning it felt like game day.

So it's 2014, in the fall, and I'm living in Los Angeles, California, playing for the LA Galaxy. One of the most famous clubs in North American soccer teams. We're living five minutes from the beach, and in this particular moment, I'm not at the beach. This time, I'm sitting in a dark closet of our bedroom. I can hear my kids playing outside. I can hear my wife with my kids. I can hear the water. I want to be outside with everyone, but I can't. The reason why is because I'm battling a severe concussion. This was probably the tenth concussion of my career, at least. I took a lot of hits.

With a lot of concussions comes headaches, anxiety, irritability, sensitivity to light and noise—there's a lot of these symptoms. Literally, I couldn't be outside. I couldn't play with my kids. Couldn't go for a five-minute walk. So, the only place I really could be for the relief of all this was this dark closet. So I'm sitting there in this closet, and it's quiet, it's cool, for the relief of the headaches and all the symptoms.

So, I'm sitting there, and when you're in a room and it's dark, you start reminiscing. You start thinking about the past. In particular, I'm sitting there thinking about this one time—the one highlight of my career.

It was about seven years ago. I was playing for a club called Burzum. It's probably one of the most famous teams in Germany—in the Bundesliga, which is probably one of the most famous and best leagues in the world. Here I am, some

Canadian kid playing in the Bundesliga. That's like a Mexican playing in the NHL—no offense. I shouldn't be there.

So, I'm playing for one of the biggest clubs in Germany. I'm sitting on the bus, and the bus rides to the games are always the most nerve racking, obviously. You're driving toward the stadium. You can see the stadium in the distance. You've got your headphones on.

I've got "Don't Stop Believing" on. Getting pumped up. The nerves are going through your body. All those thoughts: Did I eat enough, did I sleep enough, did I train enough? All these thoughts as an athlete: Are the fans going to love me? Are they going to hate me? These fears. These anxieties. These pregame jitters.

In the locker room, again I've got my headphones on listening to the music. Putting my shoes on; putting my jersey on. Coach comes in, gives his pregame speech, tries to pump everyone up. But we know how big this game is. This game's probably one of the biggest games for this club, which is one of the most traditional, historic clubs in Germany. This game means everything for the fans, for the city, for the club. So, we know how important it is. We don't care what the coach says.

So we come in; we huddle together as you do as a team. Get together. Everyone says a few words. We start walking out toward the field.

I miss that locker room.

In these large stadiums, you walk through a tunnel, and you can kind of see the fans in the distance. You can hear the stadium. The stadium's shaking—70,000 fans. And you're walking out, and you can see the opponents right next to you. It's like we're gladiators. We're walking out to war, really. It's war. It's battle. You can see the guys next to you, and you almost want to kill them. It's just…it's a war.

So we're standing there, and I still get goosebumps thinking about it. You hear the fans cheer and chant, and everyone's ready for you, and you know how big this game is.

I miss that tunnel.

So the game, it's ninety minutes. It's in the ninetieth minute, the game's zero-zero. Again, this game means everything for the club. This is one of the most important games in the history of the club. So, in the ninetieth minute, the game jitters are gone.

Throw the ball, it comes down the left side of the field. Our left wing gets it. And I knew exactly what he was going to do. I knew he was going to cross the ball and I was going to head it in the air.

I knew he was going to cross the ball, so I prepared myself.

He crosses the ball in, and literally it's like slow motion: the ball comes flying in, and it comes in, and I jump the defender. Get my head behind it—boom—goal.

I just start running around like a madman. If anybody has seen soccer highlights, you just start going apeshit like an idiot. My shirt off, everyone's jumping, crazy. One of the best feelings in the world to score a goal, especially at that moment.

I miss those games.

But the reality is, I'm in the dark closet. Literally.

I'm sitting there, and all these fears are coming down on me because I know my career's about to end. I know this concussion is the last concussion I am going to take. I never wanted my family to go through the pain that I've been going through for the last few months. Sitting in that closet every single day. So this fear, this anxiety, this pressure—everything's coming down on me at once. I just start sweating.

Then these questions start coming my way. These questions are terrifying. All these questions. These fears.

There's one question in particular that no professional athlete ever wants to face: What now?

I know the facts. I know the odds are against me. Eighty percent of ex-pro athletes are bankrupt, unemployed, or divorced after five years of their career. Depression is at an all-time high for ex-players.

I get it. I understand it now.

Because overnight you lose your passion, you lose your purpose, you lose your identity.

It's like we're just thrown off a boat into this vast ocean. Your routine's gone. Little things that you would never think about as an athlete because everything is set—your workout schedule, your eating schedule, your sleep schedule.

But now, I wake up...when do I shower?

When do I work out?

Do I work out?

What do I eat?

What am I?

Who am I?

Now what am I supposed to do?

What am I supposed to do today?

What do I do tomorrow?

What do I do next year?

It's frightening. The space is frightening. It's actually terrifying.

Now I understand why athletes are depressed after their careers. Look, I'm not trying to feel sorry for myself. I don't. Look, I have an amazing family, beautiful wife, kids. Everyone's healthy, living in one of the most amazing cities in the world.

But the reality of this unknown, scary space is the reality that I'm waking up to every day. It's without a purpose now. It's daunting. I think we've all heard athletes die twice. I've heard it before. I'm sure everyone's heard that before. I never really understood that as a player.

But I get it now. I understand it, because it's the death of your passion. It's the death of your identity. Who are you? It's gone. I'm not a pro player anymore.

What's my purpose? That's gone. I don't have a purpose anymore.

You need to go through this mourning. I've heard that, and I'm going through it. I've been through it. It's this mourning... it's difficult to understand and explain.

No one tells you about this transition.

No one tells you how hard it's going to be.

No one warns you about the fears.

No one warns you about the emptiness.

No one warns you about all these questions that you have.

What do I do with my life?

What makes my family happy?

What makes me happy?

What's my purpose?

What's my meaning?

How do I become a better man, a better husband, a better father?

It's funny, because these questions weren't relevant when I was playing. I think as a pro athlete you almost become immune to reality. Everything's great—you're a pro athlete. You're living your dream.

What's better than that? You start to become invincible. You lose focus on reality.

But now these questions are haunting me every single day.

So obviously, you reflect on this transition. Looking back on this last one and a half years since that dark closet, I can probably say I've grown more in the last one and a half years than in the past 33 years of my life.

I've challenged myself to live a more meaningful life. As cliché as this sounds, I actually stop and smell the roses. They smell great. I'm learning to be present every day with my family, my kids. Seeing the smile on my kids' faces, hearing them laugh, holding my wife's hands. Little things.

I'm learning to face these questions, rather than them terrifying me.

I'm actually finding them somewhat exciting. I'm learning to relish in this transition. I get to write a new chapter. How cool is that? I get a new chance to find a new meaning and a new purpose in life.

> Actually, I now know that I want to make a difference in life. In my life, in others, in the community.
>
> I never thought about these things as an athlete. Look, playing in front of 70,000 fans, being adored by a city, representing your country, living your dream—it's tough to beat. I know I'm never going to experience this again.
>
> Yes, I miss it. I miss it like hell.
>
> But I'm okay with it.
>
> I did it, and I'm proud as hell.
>
> Now I'm learning to wake up every single day thankful and grateful, rather than just being haunted by all these questions. I have no idea what the future holds, and I have no idea what the next chapter's going to be. The future definitely isn't clear.
>
> But for the first time in my life, I'm okay with it.

So, this was a One Last Talk from a famous professional soccer player. You might think that no one could get anything out of that talk unless they're a soccer player as well. I got on stage after Rob's talk and said:

> *Who here's a professional soccer player? Nobody. So that was a waste of time...unless of course you've ever struggled with letting something go.*

I looked around and could see the faces.

A mother who had struggled with her kids moving away.

An entrepreneur who'd sold his business.

Another person sitting there going, *Oh my God, this is my story, except that I don't have soccer cleats on.*

When you share your authentic truth, the magic for the audience is the relatability factor. They can see their own truth through the lens of somebody else's truth.

We all share the same forms of loss and pain and suffering, but the details are different. For an audience member listening to somebody else talk about their pain, they're able to connect it with their own story, whether or not they're conscious of it. They get out of their heads and get connected emotionally.

This is why it's so important to share your truth—because it's going to be very significant for someone else too.

It will let people know they're not alone.

If we don't value our own truths, we will continue to do what society has always done and continues to do: put other people on pedestals, point a finger, and say, "They're better than me. I'm not enough."

You are enough, and owning your truth is part of getting there.

1.7

The Ripple Effect of Truth: Matthew

Matthew was one of the people in the audience when Bev gave her talk. I'd invited him to give his talk already, so he knew he would be on that stage one day.

Typically, he would have gone the "aboriginal route" like Bev did at first and talked about something socially acceptable, whatever that would have been for him. But he was so moved by Bev that he ended up sharing a story about his suicide attempt.

Two weeks after he thought about killing himself, Matthew met his wife and now has three beautiful children. He doesn't have a perfect life, but it's one he would deeply regret not having. Suicide isn't even a possibility now.

As a result of Bev's talk, Matthew was also encouraged to share the recording of his One Last Talk with a relative who deals with the same type of depression and suicidal thoughts. The two had a life-changing conversation. His cousin was on the same path as Matthew and might very well have attempted suicide himself. That's now off the table for him as well.

MATTHEW'S ONE LAST TALK

In the sixth grade, I started my first business: I used to steal hood ornaments off cars and sell them to students. It was 100 percent profit—not a bad margin. I used to get a buck for Chrysler, two dollars for Cadillac, and three dollars for Mercedes.

In seventh grade, I started my second business. This was, for lack of a better term, a chop shop for bicycles that I ran out of my garage. My mom's garage. She didn't know. This was a pretty solid operation. We had three guys, and it ran like a Swiss watch. We had one guy who stole the bikes, another guy who stripped them down, and a third guy who sold the parts. That was my job.

Like any true entrepreneur, we wanted to expand operations and increase profits, but we had to find someone. The reality is, this wasn't exactly a kosher operation, right? We had to find the right person that had the tools and the talent, but also lived by an "honor amongst thieves" code.

This turned out to be pretty difficult to find. Days turned into weeks turned into months, until finally, one day, it was like fate dropped a little present into my lap in the form of a fellow seventh grader I went to school with. I was looking across campus leaving school one day, and I see this kid. His name was Big Rich, ironically enough, and he was cutting the chain off of a bike. He hopped on and pedaled away.

I'm like, "Oh shit, the plums on this kid. Broad daylight? Yeah, he's got to be part of our crew." I hopped on my bike, pedaled up next to him. I got up next to him like, "Hey, what's up, Big Rich?" He looked at me without so much as a bead of sweat on his forehead, cool as a cucumber, and said, "You want to buy my bike?" Executive decision, man—this guy was on our team. I hired him on the spot.

Within 24 hours of that decision, he got popped by the police, and he flipped on our entire crew. I got picked up, put into custody, fingerprinted, booked on larceny and all that good stuff, thus ending my illustrious career in crime. But that didn't dampen my entrepreneurial spirit. Since that time, I've started no less than seven other businesses—legitimate businesses, thank you—ranging from a boutique advertising agency to a mobile software company and everything in between.

Two common threads have been at the forefront of every single business I've started:

Number one was the pursuit of money. How much money can I make?

Number two was ignoring my passions.

In hindsight, I can tell you that this decision, this approach to business and starting companies ultimately landed me in a lot of places that I didn't want to be.

Jail, for instance, is one of those places.

I want to tell you about a couple of others.

In my 20s and early 30s, I pretty much lived in a state of constant depression. Now, growing up, I had a lot of confidence issues stemming from a combination of being short and out of shape, coming from a broken home, growing up dirt poor, and just an overall feeling of being a little bit different and never really fitting in.

Because of these confidence issues, I started making decisions about my life and my future based on fear and self-doubt disguised as practicality or chasing money, however you want to word that. It seemed like I didn't have to look very far to get advice. Everyone had it—society, family, friends, parents. Everyone had advice about what I should do for my future, what path I should take.

I listened because I didn't have confidence, right? I wasn't going to lean into my passions. Instead, I was going to listen to other people because they had to know better. I trusted everyone except myself to make decisions about my life.

I never really asked or questioned where it was that I was heading. I just put on my blinders, followed the breadcrumbs, and never really looked back.

I can tell you, in hindsight, I understand now that a lot of this advice was nothing more than other people's limitations, their own fears and beliefs just kind of projecting on me. Again, because of my confidence issues, I still just listened to all of it.

During that time, on my best days I was numb. These days were few and far between. Most days I just lived in constant depression, self-hatred, and self-loathing. I just really didn't like where my life was.

It didn't matter what I accomplished. I looked past it to the next empty goal. It didn't matter how much money I made.

To be fair, I made some money in my day, but it was never enough. It didn't matter who I was with, I would've rather been by myself, at home, curled up in a fetal position. I just couldn't figure out how to be happy. That was the second place that chasing money over meaning led me to.

The third and final place I want to tell you about was a skyscraper in downtown Detroit called the Guardian Building. This was about ten years ago. As far as buildings go, it's nice enough. The exterior is just kind of brick and limestone and tile. It's when you go through the lobby doors that you realize how special this building is. It's beautiful. It has a 150-foot long lobby, a three-story vaulted ceiling, marble column pillars, and everywhere you look, it's carved marble or mosaic tile work. They brought in a group of like ten artists to paint these amazing, vibrant murals on the ceiling. It's all finished off by this really ornate gold leafing work. It's absolutely breathtaking.

On this particular day, I wasn't there for the whole visual appeal of it. No, this day was kind of the final reminder that I disappointed myself. That I was living someone else's life, and I wasn't living my dreams.

One thing that probably makes sense to mention is the original artist who did all the gold leafing work in that building was my great-grandfather. He actually lived his passions. I'm an artist and a writer. These are my passions—what I believe I was put here on this planet to do.

Yet I've spent the majority of my life running from these passions like the plague. As I sat there in the lobby, silently admiring the artwork of other great artists, I made the decision that I was going to kill myself.

Without so much as a plan, I just stood up, I walked over to the elevators, and took them as high up as I could go. From there,

I made my way through some stairwells and stairs. I eventually found myself on the rooftop.

It's funny—you remember weird little things about a day that significant in your life. I remember the sound the pea gravel underneath my feet made as I walked toward the ledge. I remember how hard my heart was beating—so hard that I could actually feel it in my throat and my ears.

Along the entire perimeter of the roof is a three-foot wall. As I climbed up on top of it, I was really, really careful—which, if you can find irony in a situation…right?

As I stood up, I extended my arms, and I closed my eyes. At that second, the entire world just quieted down a little bit. All the city ambience and noise below were just gone. All the hustle and bustle, all of the stuff that'd been going through my head. All that stuff just quieted down. The sound of my heart beating subsided.

I experienced what I guess you'd just call peace. A sense of peace, which was a little foreign to me. I took my last breath, and I committed. I leaned forward.

I hate to do the whole spoiler alert thing, because I'm here, right? You guys are sick, you're laughing about someone talking about killing themselves!

I don't know if you chalk it up to vertigo, or dumb luck, or a guardian angel, or my subconscious just taking over. Instead of falling the 36 stories forward—the 496 feet to my death—I actually fell backward off the ledge, three feet onto my back.

As I lay there, and the shock started to wear off and the adrenaline died down and I started regaining some of my faculties, I remember thinking, "Wow, I didn't even leave a suicide note."

There would've been some people scratching their heads. But I did that for me. I know this sounds weird, but in that moment, I wasn't thinking about anyone else.

It was probably the first time in my life that I wasn't thinking about anyone else. I just wanted the pain to stop.

That was kind of the lesser-of-two-evils decision that I came up with for that day. I remember there was just this cornucopia of emotions I was going through, and feelings of shame.

How could I let things get so bad that I actually wanted to kill myself?

There was a sense of relief, because I was still there, right? Just in and out of emotions. Ultimately, the relief is what I remember the most, because I felt like I had a second chance. Like I had some hope.

I knew I had some work to do on myself—and to undo. I'm still working on myself. Ten years later, I'm still working on it.

The fact of the matter is, I may not have died that day, but a part of me that needed to go went over that ledge.

There are three places that chasing money over meaning led me to: jail, a state of depression, and literally the edge of a building trying to take my own life. Now I want to tell you a few places that I've found myself since then by paying no attention to money and only listening to what was in here.

One week. One week after that I met a cute girl, and I later found myself standing at an altar, getting ready to spend the rest of my life with her.

On three other separate occasions, I found myself standing next to that same girl in the hospital as she gave birth to each one of our kids.

I find myself here today with you to tell this story. Had I succeeded ten years ago in killing myself, I wouldn't be here.

My beautiful daughter, Lily—she's so spirited and smart, and she wouldn't be here. My son, Declan, always has a smile on his face, hilarious kid—he wouldn't have existed, or the newest addition to my family, my little baby, Finnegan. I would have deprived the world, my wife, myself of these amazing little creatures—all because I didn't listen to what was in here.

To be clear, I'm not saying money is bad, by no means. I wouldn't mind a little bit more of it. I'm not picking on entrepreneurship, either. I'm just saying, "Get the order right."

For me, I'm a husband, and I'm a father. Actually, before that, I'm an artist and I'm a writer, then a husband and father. Further on down the road, I'm an entrepreneur.

When I was a kid, my grandfather used to say he'd never seen a hearse pulling a U-Haul yet. When I was a kid, I didn't really grasp the gravity of that statement.

As I stand here today with you, I get it. He was saying, "Passions over possessions. Meaning over money."

The fact of the matter is, I don't make as much as most of you in here, but I will tell you what I do make.

I make my wife laugh every day.

I make damn sure each one of my kids knows I love them unconditionally.

I'm now making sure I am a little more true to myself, a little kinder to myself, a little more compassionate to myself.

I believe that myself and all of you—everyone on this planet— we're all put here to make a difference in this world in our own unique way.

I believe that's what I now make. Thank you.

I've dealt with quite a few people who've had suicidal thoughts, and so many of them think they are alone. So, I'll do this exercise:

When I'm doing group work, I'll ask everyone to commit to closing their eyes, and really keeping them closed. Then I'll ask them to raise their hand if they've ever had suicidal thoughts.

Typically, 60 to 70 percent of the room will raise their hand.

Then I'll have them put their hands down and open their eyes, and tell them, "More than half of you raised your hands."

A lot of people in society have had thoughts of suicide, and there's a shame that comes with that. It could be because they feel unhappy, but they don't have a place to admit they're unhappy or the guilt and the shame that comes with admitting you're unhappy when you've got kids or you've got a husband or you've all this wealth. They think they aren't even allowed to think that, which of course makes everything worse.

I think it's staggering how many people in society have suicidal thoughts. It is staggering how many people feel lonely and isolated in society today. So many people think about suicide, yet it's discussed so rarely.

This is true for so many people, whether they have suicidal thoughts or not. They feel their pain is so unique. They think it's so damaging and different that no one could understand.

They use this as an excuse to not share it.

And even if they do share it, they don't think they could have the same results.

The reality is that the pain is the same. The circumstances are different—whether it's the person who has experienced sexual abuse or the dyslexic person sitting in school or who almost committed suicide because they felt weren't useful to society.

People sometimes say to me, "Yeah, I know you're good at coaching, but my stuff is different."

They're basically saying that their pain is so unique that no one else in the world could understand them.

That's just not true.

We are all humans, we all go through the same stuff.

Your details are different, yes, but your truth is universal. Even with suicide.

This is why I asked Matt to give his One Last Talk. He had dealt with all these issues. He'd gone through some of the most common problems as it relates to suicide; yet he thought he was alone. He wasn't. His problem was so common.

Matt felt like a failure. He felt like he wasn't really contributing to humanity, he wasn't making an impact in the world—yet after he did his One Last Talk and shared it, it not only changed his life, it changed the lives of so many people around him.

For example, he had a family member reach out to him and admit that they were considering suicide, and through that discussion ended up taking a completely different path in their life.

This is how it works. We use our pain for a purpose, and it not only saves us, it helps others as well.

Your Greatest Gift Lies Next to Your Greatest Pain: Neely

By doing the work and sharing your One Last Talk, you will connect with yourself in ways you've never been able to before.

Without doing that work—whether it's in this framework or another one—you'll never fully connect with who you are.

You'll spend your life running around trying to connect with other people instead. You'll assume money is the problem, or that you don't have the right girlfriend, or that your house isn't big enough, or that your job isn't meaningful enough. You'll find answers that you think validate the pain you feel.

But when you share your One Last Talk, as long as it's truly authentic, you actually fall in love with yourself (as corny or cliché as that may sound). You connect with yourself at a level you never have before. You begin to accept yourself in a way that you never have before.

A great example of this is Neely. When I met Neely, there was no doubt that she was talented. She's got a very quiet presence, but I always had this sense that a large part of her was hiding. It was in the shadows.

She ended up coming on a retreat with me, and bit by bit, she would take down her defenses. The big thing she kept saying (like many people) was, "I just need to find my passion. I need to find my calling. I need to find my thing."

In other words, she wanted to uncover the thing that lies in the future. As though it were outside of her.

So, I asked her one day, "How is your quest going? Did you check under that rock over there? Your passion might be under it. You never know where you might find it."

I was kidding with her of course, but part of the joke was pointing out a truth: she kept phrasing it as though her passion were something outside of her.

I don't see it that way. My view is it's already inside of her (and everyone). Your job is not to "discover" it outside of you. Your job is to find it inside of you and then let it out.

The way I often explain this is to talk about the difference between a talent and a gift.

A talent is something you can do really well. A gift is something you are born with or developed very early.

The problem is that we mix gift in with passion, which doesn't make sense. You can be passionate about things, like Harley-Davidsons or painting or wine. I have a friend who is like this with wine. He knows everything about wine. He studies it, learns about it, revels in it. When he talks about wine, he lights up. You can see his passion. He buys and enjoys expensive wine for himself and his family. He buys wine to share with friends (and on the odd occasion, every ten years or so, he buys me a bottle of wine).

But a gift is something that you have inside of you. It's not been given to you. A gift is something you have, inside of you, and your job is to *give your gift to the world*.

If you don't give it away, the world misses out, you miss out, and you don't fully show up in the world.

For Neely—and for most people—*her greatest gift lies right next to her greatest pain*.

She avoided that for years, because to unlock her gift meant she had to face her pain.

When I asked her to speak at One Last Talk, she froze. I knew she had it in her. I knew she had to share it to move forward, but I wasn't sure if she knew that.

She eventually said, "I'm ready. I want to speak my truth." This is what she said.

NEELY'S ONE LAST TALK

I was on the wrong side of a door that I could not open, no matter how hard I tried.

I was led to a basement room in the neighboring house, for a very different reason than what I originally thought. And there was this really cool toy in the corner. It kind of looked like one of those build your own rollercoaster things that you could piece together.

I remember looking at it, being like, "Oh my God. That's so cool. And it's weird that it's so dark in here, but that's pretty cool."

And then something felt really off. So, I started to walk for the door.

And I remember seeing the light under the door and reaching for the door handle. And I began to tug on it, but a hand stopped me. And it was much stronger than mine.

And then I really knew something was wrong.

And then I began to feel tugging on my pants and on my clothes, and I couldn't hold that either.

I started screaming, screaming…one of those screams where you're afraid you'll never be heard.

And then I just stopped and looked to the corner and thought, "Why can't I just play with the cool toy?" I just wanted to play with the toy.

And then, everything kind of blacked out.

My next memory is of my mom sitting on her knees and looking into my face, shaking and crying, and saying, "Please tell me what happened. Please tell me what happened to you." I told her in the best way I could. Being a young kid and having that kind of vocabulary, you can't quite understand or describe what happened to you.

Shortly after, my mom took me to see a therapist, which as a kid looks like playing with awesome toys and dollhouses. The therapist comes back and says, "Don't worry, there's no long-term trauma. She's gonna be okay. But I have to report the abuser."

And my mom got very panicked, and said, "Please don't. Please don't report my nephew."

The therapist was legally obligated to do so, and so she did.

After that, life went on. And no one really talked about it. I should say, no one talked about it period. Christmases came with a spoonful of avoidance, trying to not be in the same room, and I obediently would take photos next to him and smile and pretend like things were okay, like everybody else. I kind of just put this memory in a box and labeled it. Maybe it could be a bad dream. Is it possible I could just keep it there?

Then I got into my teens and the memories started bubbling up again. I couldn't make it go away. It came time that I needed to get some confirmation that it actually happened. I don't know if it was a combination of just starting to understand my sexuality…I was sixteen years old. I had a boyfriend at the time. And so I brought it up, and my mom confirmed it.

For whatever reason, I called my boyfriend shortly after and told him about the conversation that I had just had. He called me a liar, which was shocking at first.

Then he said, "You told me that you've never done that sort of thing with a guy."

Like I had a choice.

He wanted to know every detail, which was very difficult to describe. And when I got to the point of blacking out, he was very adamant about wondering whether or not I had actually been raped.

And at the time, I was like, "You know, I don't really know." And that was an even bigger freak out. After that, I didn't talk about it again.

And yeah, life went on.

I noticed that somebody very important to the story wasn't showing up, which was my dad. And by the time I had reached my mid-20s or so, enough was enough as far as going to these family Christmases and holidays and pretending that things were okay. Especially because my family member who violated me was still there.

And so, I sat my dad down on our back porch, and said, "I'm done. I'm done going to these family gatherings. That thing that happened when I was young, I don't know if you know that this really affects me."

And he said, "What am I supposed to tell everybody?"

"I don't know. You can tell 'em whatever you want. I'm just not coming."

And to be truthful, that was a huge relief, just saying that.

I had brought it up, but the conversation wasn't over. Coming up to this point, I had been becoming a little bit more of myself, a little more myself, a little more myself, and letting my dad see that.

We kind of have a fundamental difference in beliefs, and that's always been an issue as well, but underneath that has been this whole idea of this never really feeling like he had my back—and was in fact putting me into situations where it was more likely to happen again. One summer, he hired my cousin to mow our lawn. I loved to be outside, but those days…those were inside days. So the conversation didn't feel over, and it still probably isn't over.

But one particular evening, I was sharing a piece of myself with my dad, and it snowballed into him saying, "Okay, why are you hanging onto this? Can you just let this go? Why can't you just be part of this family?"

And I tried to explain the best way I could without being like, "Isn't it obvious?" But he started to get really angry with me, and he said:

"Do you honestly think he would do that to you now? Like, do you even know how old he was when that happened? And don't you think I would have stopped it had I seen it?"

It was devastating to hear that from a parent.

But it was what I needed to hear to really understand there was only one person that I needed to acknowledge the story, which was me.

The people in my life who were closest to me, in one way or another, kept telling me to forget.

> And I can't forget.
>
> And I won't forget.
>
> I am here, acknowledging it to myself and to you guys—many of whom are friends, dear friends—and to the world that this happened, and it impacted me.
>
> I need to do this to actually move forward, because I've got some pretty cool shit to do.
>
> Thank you.

The response to her speech was overwhelming. Almost immediately, a woman stood up and said this:

As a fellow survivor of childhood sexual abuse, I just wanna commend you for sharing your story. And I'm much older than you. And just to tell you to keep talking about it because in every part of your life, it will come into play. So just continue to talk about it. Don't be afraid to talk about it with the people that are important in your life. Don't be afraid of...I don't know if you have children yet, but don't be afraid, because things will come up for you.

And not only that, but my wife Pauline stood up and shared something she had never talked about publicly before to a group of people:

So, I was raped years ago, when I was eighteen years old.

And I never told anyone—not a soul.

And I was really ashamed and embarrassed about that. I blamed myself. And so, just in the last number of years, I've told people. And in the last couple of months, just before Christmas, I think it was, Philip put it on Facebook, with my permission of course.

And I had told some members of my family, but not all. And it was really interesting the reaction from people. Some people that I didn't know and friends on Facebook just rushed in with so much love. Not everyone in my family reacted well, but that's their choice.

The point is, personally sharing it has really lightened me, and I feel better. So, I would encourage anyone in the room who's gone through that or something similar, male or female, I would think about sharing, if you can.

I know I wouldn't have shared this today, in public, without Neely's courage.

Neely, your talk touched me. So, thank you.

That's why we do this.

Because when you free your truth and speak it to another, it helps you, but it also gives other people permission to share theirs.

Yes, this was at an event, but it's not just about the audience there that day. There's going to be somebody who's going to read this book or watch Neely's video on YouTube, and they're going to realize, "Wow, I'm not alone."

And maybe they will go further. They'll think, *I'm not alone. Maybe my truth matters. Maybe I matter. What would it be like if I shared my story with two people, ten people, 170 people...or the world?*

It's your truth—but it's not just about you.

We share because, through sharing what we have experienced and helping others who are going through something similar, each of us has the ability to ultimately remove pain in the world.

Your pain has a purpose, and that purpose is to help you find and unlock your gift and give it to the world.

And that is why we do this and why it continues.

That's why One Last Talk exists.

And that is why I am inviting you to speak your truth.

PART

HOW ONE LAST TALK CAN HELP YOU SPEAK YOUR TRUTH

TWO

2.1

What Is One Last Talk?

One Last Talk is an invitation to find your truth and speak it out loud to at least one person, and it's the framework to help you do it.

2.2

Why Is It Called One Last Talk?

Unless I set the frame that this is literally their last talk ever, people won't go deep enough.

If it were Your First Talk, well then there'd be no urgency. There'd be no need to go deep. It's just the first one. You can always go deep later.

Once you tell people that this is their One Last Talk, it challenges them. It focuses the mind and opens the heart by making them face death, even if it's only a metaphor for death.

These are talks that people have usually never shared before, and the frame of death—of finality—is what gets them there.

2.3

How Does One Last Talk Work?

There is only one instruction for constructing a One Last Talk:

> *If you had One Last Talk to give before you left this planet, what would you say, and who would you say it to?*

There is also a set of rules for the Speaker and the Listener.

SPEAKER RULES

- Fifteen minutes (or less).
- No slides or visuals.
- You must speak YOUR truth in the speech—no one else's.

- Your talk must be based on your personal experience and your feelings only.
- No prescriptive elements (e.g., "Here are four easy steps to change...").
- No advice (e.g., "You need to do this...").
- No preaching or moralizing (e.g., "You should feel this way...").
- No virtue signaling (e.g., "Look at these schools I built in Cambodia...").
- You must deliver the talk to at least ONE other human (in person, if at all possible).

LISTENER RULES

- No interruptions.
- No judgment.
- No questions.
- When the talk is finished, tell the speaker what you are going to do differently in your life because of what you heard in the talk.

That's it.

2.4

How Do I Discover My One Last Talk?

You walk through the exercises in Part III. If you do those, you should come to the end with a pretty clear One Last Talk idea.

Here's the thing to remember: this process is not really about choosing your talk.

It's more about uncovering your talk.

A lot of people have this perception that I pull all this stuff out of people—that I discover their hidden secrets.

I don't. I'm not that good. I don't believe I've ever discovered anything about anyone. All I've done is held a mirror to people. I just help people see things that are right there in front of them, that have always been there, that they're trying to ignore.

The real key to finding what you need to say is deeply connecting with your most painful memory, pain point, or moment that you went through that you want to avoid the most. That's usually the place to start.

Once you can think of that, ask yourself, "Do you wish you had heard a talk around that memory that might have helped you to deal with that pain better than you have so far? What are the words you needed to hear when you were in that situation?"

Start with the visceral moment. The thing you remember the most.

Then think about what that moment meant to you.

Finally, you want to ask what the hope is at the end—how you came out of it—which ends up being the basis for your talk.

But in this step, you want to ask yourself, "What would I have wanted or needed to hear in order to help process the pain?"

We're very focused on avoiding pain and fear, but this

isn't about avoidance. It's about processing the pain by accepting it.

There is a great Buddhist saying: "Pain is inevitable, but suffering is not."

What that means is that pain will happen to you. You can't ever get away from that. But you can stop suffering from that pain if you face it, process it, and move through it.

And you can find a purpose in that pain if you share it to help others.

That's essentially what One Last Talk is all about.

2.5

Why One Last Talk Matters to You

When I talk about One Last Talk and why it matters, I like to use the example of a fictitious woman in Yellowknife, which is a small, isolated town in northern Canada, in the middle of nowhere.

I usually call her Peggy.

Peggy has had a hard life.

She can't afford therapy, and even if she could, there aren't really any therapists around her. And of course, she doesn't have the means to get on a plane and go to Toronto or Boulder or Austin and experience a live One Last Talk event.

In fact, Peggy will never have access to many of the things that most of us take for granted. Peggy will have to struggle and fight for everything she gets her whole life.

Yes, the odds are stacked against Peggy.

But it's not hopeless.

And she hasn't given up.

Yes, she's been judged, and she's judged herself her whole life.

She's tried to bury it...but deep down, she feels like she has something to say. A truth to speak that desperately needs to get out.

She just needs some help.

It won't take much. She can do almost all the work herself. She just needs a tiny bit of direction and a little loving push.

I will probably never meet Peggy, but I wrote this book so Peggy will know that she's not alone.

That she has help.

I want this book to stir her. To wake the courage she has in her.

I want her to question—for maybe the first time—whether her truth might matter.

Even if she has a hard time accepting that it matters for her, maybe she can see that it will help others.

And this book will give her the direction she needs. And maybe the loving push.

To uncover, accept, and speak her truth.

You probably don't live in Yellowknife.

Your name is probably not Peggy.

But you have an unspoken truth in you.

I believe your truth matters.

And I think, deep down, you believe that too.

I am inviting you speak it.

This is where you start.

PART

HOW TO UNCOVER YOUR TRUTH

THREE

What if I'm Scared?

At this point, you might want to do it, but you might also be thinking:

This sounds really hard. I'm afraid. I don't know if I want to do this.

I get it. Working through this process was the hardest thing I've ever done in my life.

This is just an invitation. It's an invitation to get to something you don't fully know is there yet but that you can probably feel.

Here's the thing: it's not as hard as you think it is.

Well, I shouldn't say that.

Yes, it IS hard to uncover and speak long-held truths.

But when you think of this with a broader perspective, it seems much easier.

If you think about the cost of not doing it—the hard life you will have, harder than the hard life you have now because you haven't done this work—it doesn't seem that hard in comparison.

When you have a long-term perspective, it's not hard to do the work.

I would go so far as to say that if you do not in some way face the hard and painful truths of your life, you won't ever fully live.

The world will never fully see you, and you will never fully see yourself or get in touch with your real gift.

In short, without speaking your truth, you'll never fully show up.

I don't want to sell it.

I don't want to push anybody into this.

If you're not ready, that's fine. Don't do it.

You have to decide to do this for yourself in order for it to work.

That being said, I am not going to let you just run away.

So many people use their kids or society or people around them as an excuse not to do the work. But I'll just use those very things to motivate them to do it.

I'll give you an example, from my own family:

When my wife was considering doing a One Last Talk, she kept making excuses and finding reasons not to. I could have gotten blue in the face trying to convince her. But none of that would have worked.

She'd never do it for herself.

So I said, "Think of Maggie [our daughter], but forty years from now. What would you want for her?"

She looked and me, and said, "Well that's not fair."

I said, "I don't care whether or not it's fair. *What would you want for Maggie?*"

With tears rolling down her face, she said, "Well, of course

I'd want her to do this. She'd need to in order to look after herself."

"Well, what kind of message are you sharing with Maggie by not doing that for yourself now?"

Yes, that was a low blow. But this is my family. You're damn right I am going to make sure we all do our work.

Pauline did her One Last Talk, and she is deeply grateful that she did. In fact, she wishes she went deeper (she discusses this more later, in her own voice).

If you're afraid, that's okay. So was I before mine, and so was Pauline before hers.

Fear is good.

It means you're probably going deep into your emotions.

The way to beat the fear is to recognize it, accept it, and give the talk anyway.

That is courage.

Don't go to your deathbed wondering, *What did I miss? Did I really show up the best way I could?*

I don't want you thinking when you're 96, *Hey where's that book? I know I need to go through the process now.*

Don't carve it into your gravestone: *I'll do better next time.*

No.

Now is the time.

3.2

The Biggest Blocks to Delivering a One Last Talk

Before we get into the exercises to help you uncover the truth you want to speak, here are a few common blocks that people encounter as they start this work.

I am not telling you because I want you to avoid these issues.

If anything, I want you to lean into them.

I don't know what emotions you'll feel, but when they come—and they will—recognize them, accept them, and then use them as your guide to help you move past them.

ANGER

Anger is probably the biggest block that most people face in their lives. Fear is a kitten next to anger.

The problem with anger is it's internalized and is not addressed. And always the anger is directed at a person. It's directed at person for the things they've done or the things they've not done.

Anger is so very, very destructive. When people are angry, they see the world completely differently.

Here's the biggest stumbling block with anger. None of us want to experience it. None of us want to feel it. None of us want to talk about it. So, we internalize it.

Often, people will sit in front of me and they'll say they're not angry, and I'll say, "When was the last time you got angry?"

And they go, "Oh god, somebody cut me off in traffic yesterday, I almost ripped their face off."

And I go, "Well, what happened? Where do you think anger came from?"

"Oh, it just came out of me. I'm not an angry person, it just came out."

I say, "Where did it come out of, your ass or your pocket or your backpack?"

They look at me confused. But the fact is, it came out of you, so it's an expression of you.

Yes, the button was pushed by somebody cutting you off, disrespecting you, threatening you, annoying you, but ultimately, it exposed the anger that is already there.

I often talk about this in relation to One Last Talk. If someone is on stage, you don't want them to be delivering a speech with an angry charge.

They need to have first processed their darkness and pain in order to serve anybody. If they say, "Well, it's my One Last Talk, so I need to rip the bandage off and share the darkest moment of my life," but they haven't done the work of processing to see the value in what they're sharing, it will be of no value to anyone else either.

They're putting current anger into the memory. They think, "I'll do that. Sounds like a bit of fun." And then when they deliver their talk, you can feel the angry charge.

That's a catastrophe.

It reminds me of the Buddhist proverb, "Holding onto

anger is like grasping a hot coal with the intent of harming another; you end up getting burned."

You don't want to give your One Last Talk from a position of anger.

If you feel anger as you do these exercises, that's okay. It might even be good, as it probably means you are doing some real emotional work.

But sit with the anger first. Process it. Try to understand it before you turn away from it or use it as energy to propel you.

Here's an example of why you can't do this from a position of anger, and how unprocessed anger corrupts the process:

I was doing some couples work at a retreat, and one woman shared a story about how she was laying on the bathroom floor, balled up in excruciating pain, and her husband came into the bathroom, stepped over her, brushed his teeth, gargled his mouthwash, spit it out, stepped back over her, and walked out the door and went to work without even asking about her.

Her husband was shocked by this, "That's not true at all. I never did that!"

The following day, she apologized to the group. She admitted that she'd made this story up. She was so enraged by anger—specifically anger that she'd never dealt with—that she made this story up.

As we dove deeper with them, it was quite clear that her story was a true expression of how she felt with him. *She felt like she was in constant pain and completely unseen.* The event that she made up was a realistic expression of her emotion—it just never actually happened in reality.

Recognizing this led her to be able to open up to him, and together they made some great progress.

The point is, if you approach your One Last Talk from a position of unprocessed anger, you will end up letting it take you astray. If, as you work through these exercises, something just comes out of the blue—a memory or something that you had been unwilling to face in your new truth—and it hits you hard, then don't rush into your One Last Talk.

You don't want to do this from a position of dismay, numbness, anger, judgment, blame, or any of those things. Feel your anger first, process it and work through it, then talk about it in a One Last Talk.

If you are still very angry—and I mean raw, unprocessed anger—but you still think you want to give a One Last

Talk, there are three things I would ask to help you see if you are ready.

I would begin by challenging you about whether you were ready to share it. When I say ready, I mean *is it the right timing?* It may not be, and that is fine.

The second thing would be that I would ask if there is anything you can do to kind of lessen the anger—diffuse it a little bit. Is there a conversation that you need to have? Is there some unfinished business around it that perhaps you haven't addressed to kind of lean into it a little bit more? If that's the case, I'd maybe journal a little bit about it. The more you can connect with it, the more it loosens its grip on you.

You're not trying to get rid of it, because that's not the goal. The goal is just for it to not control you.

Then the final piece is that I would ask you to share the story a little bit more—a few times. Speak about it a few times. Share it a few times with yourself first and become comfortable with the fear to the point where it's not gone, just reduced.

If you are still struggling with raw, unprocessed anger, it might be because you have not honored it. You've never truly stepped into the feeling, the uncomfortableness, the lack of control that we often feel when we get angry.

I think the problem is, we get out of control with our anger when it's not actually addressed.

When you consider anger—typically when it comes to other people like our parents, our friends, our family, our loved ones—the way people deal with it is to say things like, "Well, they did the best they could," and, "They didn't mean it," and, "They've apologized."

And we say things like, "We've forgiven them," and we think then the anger is gone with the forgiveness.

Ultimately, if anger is not addressed, it comes back to haunt you. It's almost like a sense of revenge. You will find a way to express your anger, whether it's in their face aggressively or whether it's passive aggressively, and it always comes out. It always oozes out eventually or else it blows up in one thing.

Here's the magic: when you can separate the person from the behavior, it allows you to isolate the challenges; it allows you to express anger as it relates to the behavior but not to the essence of the person.

I like to use the glasses example to teach this. I will show a client a glasses case and say, "This is the person."

Then I'll open up the glasses case, take out the glasses,

and say, "This is the behavior. It's okay to be angry at the behavior."

Then I'll show them the glasses case in my other hand and say, "It's okay to continue to love the person."

So you can love the person, but you don't have to like their behavior, and that is a way for us to address and to feel, to connect with anger, and in isolation and independence without feeling this level of disloyalty, and uncertainty, and confusion as it relates to the person.

FEAR

I often use this quote in my work: "Fear is the assassin of dreams."

When people are scared to do One Last Talk, I say, "Great. What are you scared of? A talk? No. What are you really scared of? Let's go a bit deeper."

I've heard public speaking is the number one fear in the world, but that just doesn't land for me.

I will admit, I fear speaking. Every time I speak, I want to puke.

But at some point, I asked myself how I would feel about speaking if I just did it myself instead of in front of others.

I sat with that for month and realized something really simple:

It's not the actual speaking I'm afraid of.

We can't use the excuse anymore that public speaking is our biggest fear, on the same level as being burned to death or being buried with spiders or snakes. Here's what the truth is:

You're not afraid of public speaking.

You're afraid people in the room will not like you.

You're afraid people in the room will judge you.

Taking this one step further: **we're all ultimately afraid that people will not accept us.**

Most of this fear is about acceptance.

So, what we tend to do is manipulate the talk, manipulate the conversation, manipulate the outcome to get it to the point where we think people will like us best.

But when we finally let go of this—when we let go of our fears and our need to be accepted—we get out of our own way and let our truth come out as it really is.

Even though we want connection more than anything, we use fear as an excuse.

So, I'm sick of the fear conversation.

I'm not saying it doesn't exist. It does.

We all say, "Well I'd love to climb the mountain, but I'm afraid of heights."

You need to ask the deeper question.

Why are you afraid of heights?

The answer isn't just that you've always been afraid.

What's beyond that?

What's below that?

What are you really afraid of?

Digging into that is the core of One Last Talk.

I remember my biggest fear ever as a speaker. My buddy Jeff asked me to be his best man for his wedding. When he asked me to be his best man, I initially answered, "Oh my God, absolutely."

I didn't get a lot of recognition in life. I never won anything. I was never really seen in the world. I wasn't really asked to do cool stuff, so when you're given an invitation like that, it's very exciting.

All of that happened in about two and a half seconds. Then I remembered this meant I had to give a speech.

I was petrified. *Oh Christ, I wanted recognition, and now it means I've got to stand on a stage? Oh, bloody hell, no!*

He took me to show me the venue, and I walked into the room...which is in a hotel...which has an old theater. Lo and behold, there's a stage. A full-on stage.

The minute I walked in, I knew in my heart and soul. I knew.

"Jeff, where do the speeches take place?"

All chipper and happy, he says, "On the stage, Philip. Won't it be great!"

I thought I was going to vomit all over the antique carpet.

I decided I had to get out of it. I was literally going to break my own leg if I had to. Picturing how I would jump off this stage and hurt myself—any way to try to get out of this thing.

That was a few weeks before the wedding. I found myself getting toward the wedding, and of course I went into that very heady space of trying to protect myself. *How do I protect myself?*

I said to myself, "Well, if I get up there and I'm really funny, that'll be cool, because I can insult everybody. I can try to be funny, tell bad jokes. People can judge me or whatever, but at least I'll be safe."

Then I realized, "Okay, that's not going to work. I'm not funny at all!"

"Well, what if I just try to be super intelligent, or a combination between the two?" So, I spent all my time before the wedding writing up the smartest, cleverest speech I could. I worked so hard on making it perfect.

The day of the wedding, I looked at it, and I knew.

It was an awful speech, and I knew it.

I got up on stage, so nervous I had sweated through my tux before I'd spoken a word. I think I told a few bad jokes, and I don't know what happened or how I switched, but at one point in the speech, I just let go.

I threw the note cards away and I spoke my truth about Jeff and how great he is to people and how sometimes I take him for granted. I just spoke. I just shared my truth and spoke really deeply from my heart, from a very vulnerable, real space. From a place of pure love. I kind of teared up a little bit.

Then I said thanks to the bride and groom, and as I started walking off stage, I realized that everyone was crying.

I knew why everyone was crying, *I just fucked up the wedding. Like I've just screwed up the whole wedding. Oh God, I'm a failure again.*

But then, out of nowhere, I got this overwhelming, immediate standing ovation.

I was not prepared for that (people were not drunk at that point, either, because it was early in the day). You don't get standing ovations at Irish weddings, historically. I didn't know what to do.

People were hugging me and kissing me, and this young

guy walked straight up to me. I've never seen him before, never seen him since. I didn't know who he was—a complete stranger. He walked up to me, and he said:

"Man, that was amazing. If I ever get married, will you be my best man?"

To which I looked him straight in the eye and said, "Will you go fuck yourself!"

He started laughing. He hugged me and said, "You have got a gift."

At that moment, it certainly stirred something in me. It's often strangers who can see something in us that we can't or do not want to see in ourselves.

My truth was—and is—that this is what I am here to do.

I'd love to tell you that the Hollywood story was that the following morning I set up my speaker website, got a speaker agent, and started speaking.

It was seven or eight years later before I spoke to those kids in the school and was finally carried kicking and screaming toward the very thing I want to do on this earth for the rest of my life.

That is what fear does to us. Don't let it hold you back any longer.

If you're scared, it's because you're focusing on the wrong person. Don't make this journey about you. Make it about the one person who needs to hear your message. It might be a loved one. It might be a stranger. But one thing is for certain: if your talk inspires one single person, it's worth it.

The ultimate destination of fear is regret. If you give every ounce of yourself on that stage, there will be no regret. If you hold back, you'll always wonder, *What if?*

The depth of joy and growth you'll feel from giving your talk is in direct proportion to the vulnerability, honesty, and courage you're willing to bear on stage. Simply put, the more you unconditionally give of yourself, the more you'll receive.

So, do yourself (and everyone in the audience) a favor: leave it all on that stage. You'll be glad you did.

REGRET

People have a lot of regrets. They have self-judgment and self-directed anger around these regrets. But they often can't connect with them, let alone discuss them.

Regret is almost always about judgment. They're afraid of what it would mean to face their regrets because they judge themselves so much for them.

We have a very sadistic relationship with regret. We hold onto it as a mechanism to beat ourselves up, to hold ourselves down, and to hold ourselves to a higher standard than is reasonable.

This is because of something I have a saying about: "We give ourselves what we feel we deserve."

When you don't feel you deserve success or happiness, you pass up opportunities for it. Then you beat yourself up because of that. It's this vicious cycle that people get into.

I have a client, Chris, who was in a job he did not like. If he stayed for another four years, he was set to make a million dollars in bonuses. But he made what he thought was a rash decision, quit, and left all that money on the table. He just could not get beyond beating the hell out of himself for making that decision.

By the way, it wasn't a rash decision at all. He was utterly miserable in his job, but he did't talk about the misery and the pain and the cost of staying in a job that he hated.

He talked about leaving money on the table. That if he'd

stayed in for the four years, he would have walked away with a million dollars, but that he didn't do that. Now that he's moved on, he's using the very decision he'd judged himself on to create success in his life and other areas.

The point is that he was beating himself up for something, saying he regretted it, even though it was the best decision. He just wouldn't let go of the self-abuse that came from regretting this decision. I see so many people using regret in this way that allows them to continue to beat the shit out of themselves.

The best part about One Last Talk is that there is not a specific day you have to do this on. You don't have to regret passing this up—as long as you do it.

SHAME

Some people don't want to be seen delivering a part of their life they're ashamed of. This is because they assume everyone will be ashamed of them too.

They imagine the feeling of the closest people to them being ashamed of them, and then they multiply that by a thousand.

For this group, the biggest block is not seeing value in their truth, because they've never stopped to understand their truth. They're too busy reading everybody else's biographies and seeing those people's truths.

It's all about external judgment. We're all so obsessed by what other people think of us.

To me, shame is connected to judgment, so that's why I have kept the shame section really small. But the next section is judgment. Whenever someone talks about shame, I like to dig underneath shame and find out where the judgment's coming from.

JUDGMENT

Where judgment is present, there is no growth.

I absolutely believe that at my core. When judgment is present, there is *zero* growth.

To show that people are often unwilling to see their growth, I usually tell my daffodil story:

I was working with a person who was very judgmental of themselves. I gave them a daffodil bulb (the seed). I had them plant the bulb in the ground.

I asked them, "Can you see what you've done?"

They said, "I don't see anything. I just see mud."

I said, "You just planted a daffodil bulb."

They came back two weeks later, and the stem had burst through the soil, and there was growth and life there.

And they said, "Yeah, but no flower. Where's the flower?"

Two months later, I brought them back, and I said, "Look, there's the bulb that you planted, and it's bloomed into a beautiful yellow flower that's growing. Look what you did. You helped create that."

And they said, "Yeah, but how long will the flower last? Maybe a week? Two weeks? Then it's fucking dead!"

The flower, of course, was just a representation for their life.

I'll give you another example of how judgment corrodes:

Be honest. Did you feel judgmental toward Quan, even after reading the context around his One Last Talk?

If so, that's fine. A lot of people probably did. But let me explain how this sort of judgment hurts you:

One of the reasons we judge people very strongly in the world today is because the more we judge, the more of a psychological barrier we can create between *myself* and *them,* the better we can feel about ourselves. When we push the "other" far away from ourselves and say, "Look at that person, look at that murderer, look at that person who believes [whatever]: they are evil," it makes us feel like we are good.

They may or may not be evil. I don't know. But I do know that, when you do that, you are literally pointing away from yourself. The more we judge, the more we distance ourselves, both from others and even from ourselves.

What I have realized, both in getting to know Quan and working with other people in prisons, is that I am not so different from them. There was just a tiny space, and it was just one degree here or there between us. It was so small that I can hardly identify the line.

And that scared the shit out of me.

It also freed me in ways I didn't imagine.

I think that's why judgment is so prevalent.

We judge ourselves the same. We judge ourselves so deeply that it pushes us away from the essence of who we are. It gives us permission not to do the things we actually want to do in this world.

Judgment can come from so many places, but no matter where it comes from, here's the question I ask:

"What if you never speak your truth? What if you go to your grave holding this truth? What is the cost? Both the cost you're aware of, and the cost you might be unaware of?"

The way people respond to this is staggering.

Some people say, "It'll probably affect my ability to connect with my kids. The residual anger will always be there, and it will come out."

Others say, "If I don't get this out of my body, it's going to manifest itself physically. It's like a cancer."

People will keep trying to say they're unaware of it, but intuitively they know there's something still there.

Usually, they'll admit, "I need to get this out."

What often brings about a shift is when the person sees the exact same thing happening in somebody else. If somebody else is sitting there with the same exact issue as you, how can you honestly support them?

You've got to share your truth in order to do that.

And when you do, that person begins to think, *I'm not alone in this. There is hope.*

That's when their energy shifts, and even if they can't get there fully for themselves or even their kids, they might be able to get there for somebody else.

Again: *your pain has a purpose.* It's not just about you.

Somebody else somewhere else has suffered through what you went through, and sharing this will not just help you through it—it'll help them through it as well.

That is one way you get past your judgment. You make it about who you will help.

JUDGMENT (OF THIS BOOK)

This is another obstacle that we saw come up while editing this book. We had several people read it during the rough draft stage. Some of them were people I didn't know, had never met, and who had never heard of me. My editor and I did this because we wanted to make sure the book made sense to a person who had no background in me or my work.

While many of those people did enjoy the book and got a

lot out of it (in fact, most ended up doing a One Last Talk themselves), we found a small portion had very strong negative reactions to the book.

I can see if someone read this and it didn't resonate with them. That's reasonable, and if that's the case, no problem. This is not for everyone.

But when someone has a very strong negative reaction to this book (or anything in life), when there is a charge there, it usually means something else is going on. In essence, the book hit a nerve in that person.

There was one specifically who stood out, both for his comments and what happened afterwards. His name is Dan. Dan was highly critical of several parts of this book, and wrote long comments disagreeing with large parts of the premise.

Now, some of his comments were valid, and by addressing them, we made the book better. But some of them were highly charged in a way that I felt he was angry at something else, and "taking it out" on the book.

To his credit, even though the book obviously made Dan angry, he did not dismiss it. Dan had done enough emotional work himself to know that if he was getting angry, then maybe there was something there he needed to explore.

So, he wrote his version of a One Last Talk and delivered it to a group of 300 students at a school he teaches at.

And to Dan's surprise, it not only helped him, it sent a shockwave through the school. This is what he said in an interview with my editor:

> *When I wrote my One Last Talk and presented it in front of 300 students, I prefaced it by saying, "I know that my inner journey is important to me, but I don't know that it's important to other people. So let me tell you what I've gone through, and you all can tell me whether or not it's meaningful for you."*
>
> *I was really shocked at what happened. Afterwards, only a few people wanted to talk to me about the specifics of my journey, but what they wanted to do was open up and share with me about their journey. They felt like they could be vulnerable because they saw me do it and realized they can do that too. It's not scary.*
>
> *And the class I taught changed after that. Students started talking about a lot of the pain that they had gone through. Some students had been physically abused or sexually abused, and some students had been raped. One student wrote a piece about her father raping her. It was the first time she'd ever talked about it. This was over several weeks of course, but it was like a dam opened on the entire class.*

They came to me and they were kind of half-jokingly saying things like, "Why are you making us cry every day?" I was like, "I'm not making you do anything. I'm providing a space where you're able to actually address these feelings." Not just students, but faculty as well they came to me to talk about things they were going through.

This was so great in so many ways, seeing these kids open up and emotionally connect with me and each other, all because I stood up and told my honest, authentic truth to them.

But I am still so jarred by this. It's just so shocking to me that by telling my truth, people were able to tell theirs.

And writing it was so much harder than I thought it would be. I think part of the difficulty was how challenging it was to be truthful in everything that I was saying. And I caught myself a few times as I was writing, I would try to avoid something very painful by trying to make it more interesting.

I would think, "Well, what if the story went in this direction?" And I had to stop myself, almost yell at myself, "Why are you lying? Stop doing that! Why don't you just tell what's true and see what the response is?"

And it worked. I think what really happened, what this

book caused me to do, was to stop telling my story, and instead start telling my truth. Instead of piecing together how my story can make sense to other people, I just told them what is real and true. And that is really scary, and I think, yeah, I got kinda upset when I first realized that's what the book was asking me to do. But I did it, and it was kind of amazing.

As of the printing of this book, I have not met Dan, nor even spoken to him. My editor interviewed him and got his permission to put this into the book because I think this might be a serious obstacle for a lot of people, and I wanted them to see another person who went through this who has no connection to me.

If this book makes you very angry, maybe ask yourself why. If, as you work through the exercises, you get upset, maybe there is something there you need to look closer at.

But whatever it is, don't let it stop you from finishing your One Last Talk.

3.3

Exercise: Write Your One Last Message

The first step to giving your One Last Talk is writing your One Last Message.

It will be a message for somebody specific.

It can be for a family member—father, mother, brother, best friend, wife, or child. It can be someone you knew but haven't talked to for a long time. It can even be a message for your younger self.

It doesn't matter who you give it to. You can decide who you give it to—but it must be for a specific person.

Make it out to whomever you want and use no more than 75 words for the message. These are the only instructions:

In one or two sentences, what would be the One Last Message you'd want to share before you left this planet, and who would you share it with?

WRITE YOUR ONE LAST MESSAGE HERE:

[Or, if you prefer, go to https://onelasttalk.com/book and write your One Last Message online.]

NOTES

It is VERY IMPORTANT that you *actually write something down.*

Some of you read books that ask you to do exercises, and you never do them.

You're skeptical, or uncomfortable, or afraid, so you skip them.

I know, because I am that exact type of person: *Oh, these exercises, they're for other people, not me.*

Wrong. This isn't that kind of book.

For your own sake, there might not be anything more important than doing this work.

It doesn't have to be perfect. You can use a pencil and erase it later. That's fine.

All that matters is that you actually get a One Last Message down, on paper, right now.

If you have written something you're fine with, move to the next chapter.

If you're having issues, keep reading.

ONE LAST MESSAGE EXAMPLES

Some people need examples here, so that's fine. We'll give you a few.

Most messages are almost always very heady at first.

That's great, because it creates a significant difference from what you will create at the end.

By the end, you'll have gone from "Hey John, I love you," to "Holy shit, it's really about self-love," or whatever.

Typical generic OLM before hearing the One Last Talk speakers sound like this:

- "Fake it till you make it."
- "Work hard today; play hard tomorrow."
- "There is no try—either do it or don't."
- "You get out of life what you put in."

Some actual OLMs from One Last Talk attendees:

- "The love you want is already within you."
- "Take the time to make an authentic connection with the people you love. It's never too late."
- "Busyness won't buy happiness."
- "The more you serve yourself, the better you'll be able to serve others."
- "Follow your heart. Don't let your head or others sway how you feel."
- "I am enough."
- "Vulnerability is not weakness, and true peace comes from loving yourself and opening yourself up to real, meaningful relationships."

- "Holding on to control is like being a bird in a cage."
- "We are all perfectly imperfect just the way we are. No two of us are the same, and this guarantees that we are all special. We are life...we are love...we are all exactly who we already need to be."
- "Be true to yourself and take action in alignment with your truth."
- "It comes at a great cost, doing the work that doesn't serve you. Ask me how I know."
- "Share your gift. Hear your heart. Be your soul."
- "The purpose is in the pain. Share it, because someone needs it."
- "Allow people to love you. Create the connections that you long for."

MORE HELP: "I CAN'T COME UP WITH ONE"

If you're still having trouble, the basic excuse you're probably using—that most people use—is something along the lines of "I can't come up with one."

Of course, this is complete horseshit.

The people who say this just don't want to play the game. They're worried it won't be perfect.

If someone is insisting this is the case, I would say something like:

You don't have to do it. I didn't lock the doors. You're not handcuffed to the book. I'm not pointing a gun at you. I'm just asking you to consider playing the game.

If you're annoyed because you can't get the message right, that means something. It probably means there is an obsessive need to get it perfect somewhere in you. I know you want all your ducks in a row, but those bastard ducks never line up. And the people who wait for that to happen before executing anything in life never do.

So here you are, pissed off because you can't figure out the "right" answer to the One Last Message exercise.

There is no perfect One Last Message. So, go write what you can and move on.

MORE HELP: "I NEED MORE GUIDANCE"

No, you don't.

In our world today, everything is overprescribed. When you create a space that has few rules, it bugs people.

In fact, you might be really annoyed right now.

And that's the point.

In sessions, we will literally see people vibrate and say, "What do you mean? What do I do? I need more instructions."

They want to be handled through the process. They want the rules so they can master them and be perfect and do everything right.

But by not giving in—by insisting that they sit in this uncertainty—they get to a different place. It pushes their buttons and stirs them up.

If you are having this issue, imagine we are in a room together. I would ask, "Who's having it hard?"

You might say, "Well, what are your instructions?"

I'd say, "Oh, so it's my fault you don't have a One Last Message? You're blaming me?"

You might say, "Well, I don't know what to put."

I'd say, "Why?"

You could say, "Because there was not enough instruction. It's not clear."

I'd say, "What would make it clear?"

You might say, "Well, if you give me some questions to consider..."

I'd say, "It's your message. I'm purposely not overprescribing this because I want you to go within and search for it. Are you saying you have no message at all, for anyone?"

That usually solves it.

If you persisted, I might sometimes say, "If you don't mind me asking, what is going on here? What's coming up for you? With respect, your reaction is not about your One Last Message. You can't be getting this bent up about something this small."

Then you might say, "I struggle with emotional stuff."

Or you might say, "I'm going through a divorce at the moment, thanks."

That reaction—regardless of the specifics—is almost never about the exercise. Reactions like that come from being pissed off about something else, and something in the exercise is bringing it up.

Which is good. It means you're engaging and we're getting to the hard part.

I know this can be annoying. But if you keep with it, if you trust yourself and the process, you'll get to where you want to go.

The best way I can describe it is by telling a story about what happened on one of my BraveSoul retreats in Ireland. At the beginning of this trip, a guy said to me:

"Everyone's outside, and they're all freaking out. They don't know where to go."

No one was freaking out. He was the one who was freaking out because he didn't know what was going on, and he was a control freak. It took him four days to come off of that and be okay with not knowing.

And that's when the magic happened.

He dropped out of his head, connected with his emotions, and had some amazing realizations about his life and his identity and where he was going.

I think people overprescribe their lives for a number of reasons.

For example, people who desperately need security are the most insecure people in the world. The more somebody wants security, the more it shows how deeply insecure they are about not knowing and not having answers.

I think they're also afraid. They're scared of going within— opening a door and not knowing exactly what's on the other side. They know there are emotions on the other side, and they don't want to deal with them.

People don't trust themselves. They need a framework. They need someone to tell them what to say—the first opening word and how to finish it off and what to consider.

The easy thing here would be to give you a ten-step process and four questions to stir you up before saying, "Now do it."

But that's not what I'm going to do.

To do this, you have to trust yourself, and that is hard.

Most people don't really like who they are.

I know people may not like that idea or agree with it. But I'm telling you right now: every single person I've worked with doesn't really like at least some part of who they are—at the core.

I know, because that was my problem too.

And how can you trust somebody you don't like?

We think of trust as external, and very few people talk about trust as internal.

If you don't really like who you are—you have shame, regret, and things you haven't moved past—that's one of the greatest sources of mistrust.

Well, it's time to start trusting yourself.

How do you do that?

By doing this work.

By taking ten minutes to write down your message.

It will probably be uncomfortable. It might even be hard.

But this is literally how you build trust in your abilities and, ultimately, trust in yourself.

3.4

Life Leaves Clues: How to Find Your Future in Your Past

A lot of the work I do and most of the One Last Talks I hear are about traumas that happened to people in their past.

Not everyone likes diving back into their past. And I don't blame them. Who wants to re-live pain? After all, you can't change the past, right?

The reason to examine the past is because it gives you the freedom to understand the present and thus create your future.

No, you can't change the past—but you can change how it affects you today.

More often than not, the past has a grip on you and is dictating much of your life, whether you know it or not.

It's affecting your money habits.

It's affecting your ability to love and be loved.

For example, how many people do you know who say some version of, "I can't find somebody to love"?

I don't think that's actually the issue with most of them. I think the issue is, "I can't allow other people to love me."

By understanding the past—not just intellectually, but emotionally—we can choose to loosen the grip it has on us and free ourselves to make a new future.

The more you run from it, the more it's controlling you.

The more you face it, the more you're free.

Let me illustrate how our future is contained within our past through some stories about clients I've worked with.

NAN

Nan came to one of my events because she was searching

for a particular answer: why she wasn't getting paid for her work.

Her paintings were off the charts. She painted unicorns and all sorts of stuff. A lot of people really liked them.

At one point during the event, several people were in a room together. I immediately noticed an interesting dynamic between Nan and another woman. As soon as the other woman mentioned money, I could see Nan react physically.

I had a chance to chat with her, and in the middle of our conversation, she said, "Listen Philip, I'm here to figure out how I can get paid."

Instead of focusing on her comment, I switched gears: "Where does anger show up in your life?"

"No, no, I'm not angry," she responded quickly.

She might have been able to fool others with this. She was, after all, what I call a yoga person. She'd whisper everything. The thing is, timid people are the angriest people in the world. If you ever want to get into a room of angry people, go to a yoga class. I've offended people by saying that, but in my experience, it's true.

Nan didn't fool me. I told her I felt a lot of anger from her, and I'll never forget her response. She looked at me and said, "You know, Philip, I've watched you over the last couple of days, and you're very good at what you do. But I'm telling you right now: anger and me, you're way off. You're so way off."

I said, "Okay, let's get back to this money thing."

"Yeah, that's my single biggest issue," she repeated. "Painting is what I love to do. Paintings are my expression of myself and everything else. I just can't seem to get paid enough or sell consistently enough."

"Assuming, of course, you want money," I said.

"Excuse me?" she asked, clearly perturbed.

I repeated myself: "Assuming you really want to make money."

That's when it happened. She got so mad that she was shaking.

I asked Nan to tell me about her relationship with money. Soon enough, we were able to track it back to her childhood. Her parents had fought a lot when she was a kid, and the fights often revolved around money. On the most basic level, she felt overwhelmed by the idea of not having any money, and she was completely unaware of the reality that she'd be okay.

I also asked her how money shows up in her relationships. She was a beautiful, single woman, and I thought her answer might be revealing. Again, she quickly connected the dots and exclaimed, "Oh my God! I've found a way to sabotage every relationship I'm in when a guy places a high value on money."

All these realizations hit her at once.

I was straightforward with Nan: "You're taking out a canvas, pouring your soul onto that canvas, and then asking for what you think is the dirtiest thing in the world in exchange for it. How could it feel good to ask somebody to pay for the thing that you love with something that you hate?"

I'm not exaggerating when I say I thought she was going to vomit right on the carpet in this beautiful little castle in Ireland.

She literally curled over, and I could tell she wanted to roll up into a fetal position and never be seen again.

But by the end of the week, she was going off to help a

wealthy man in the group pick out Waterford Crystal to buy for his wife.

The point is that she was unaware of this money charge in her life. She was unaware of how catastrophic her relationship with money had been in her life and how it had created loneliness and scarcity. It affected almost every facet of her life, and she had been blind to that reality.

Sometimes people need to just have that moment of realization where it all becomes clear. That was the case with Nan. I think she, non-intuitively, was aware of her issue. I think she just needed it to become blatantly obvious. It was enough of a shift that she acknowledged her relationship with money, and therefore, it loosened its grip.

MATT

When I first met Matt, he said, "If I could get you in a room with my brother, he could do such great stuff."

I asked Matt, "Tell me about you."

He said, "I'm good. My wife and I, we're good. I work pretty hard to keep her happy."

I asked, "What do you mean?"

He said, "What do I mean by what? You know: happy wife, happy life."

I said, "Well, I'm not actually a proponent of that."

He said, "Are you saying I shouldn't work hard to make my wife happy?"

I said, "No, I'm not saying that. I'm just wondering why it's extra hard. It seems like there's an *extra* emphasis here."

He repeated himself, saying he does work really hard.

I said, "Why?"

He said, "I want to have a happy relationship."

So I asked, "What's the cost here? Is there a cost, potentially?"

He said, "No, I don't see one."

I said, "What are you afraid of?"

He said, "I don't know."

Eventually, he admitted, "Actually, I'm afraid of repeating history. I'm afraid of going through a divorce."

Again, I asked why, and he said, "That's what my parents did."

So I said, "You work extra hard to make sure that your wife is happy and doesn't leave you."

He paused: "I never saw it like that, but to some extent that's true."

I asked, "Do you find yourself compromising? Biting your lip? Not speaking your truth?"

He said, "Absolutely. All the time."

I said, "What about resentment and anger?"

He said, "Until right now, I never imagined I had it. But I have it toward myself, and honestly, I have a lot toward my wife."

The very thing that he was trying to avoid by evading it actually caused him to create it. He is heading down the road for divorce—the very thing that haunts him at his core is the thing he runs toward.

It took some hard work for Matt, but this journey created something very healthy between him and his wife. He's no longer a yes-man. He stands up for himself and takes charge of what he wants, and it's helped create a level of respect in their marriage. Matt feels seen and heard in his marriage.

JASON

A lot of people say something like, "Well, it's happened, and we shouldn't dwell on it. Let's just move on."

Good luck with that. It doesn't work to just move on. What happened in the past plays out in ways we can't even measure. That's the problem.

Jason is a good example of this. The first weekend Jason came to work with me, I told him to go buy a Harley-Davidson. His kids had every piece of plastic they could ever imagine. His wife had basically any car she wanted. But he had never bought himself anything, ever.

I said, "Let's just say you fall down the stairs and hit your head really hard. You wake up and decide you want to look after yourself. What would you do?"

He said, "I'd buy a bike."

So I told him to tell me about the bike. He said, "It's about a meditative state. Some people have fishing, or wine, or climbing. For me, it's bikes."

Apparently, as he walked out that day, somebody asked him how he thought it was going. He said, "I hope it gets better than this. All McKernan told me to do is buy a motorbike."

He ended up driving from Alberta to Illinois to pick up a custom bike. When he got close, he literally had a physical reaction. He turned around and drove back for hours until he remembered us and the accountability from the group he was in.

He pulled over, puked, and finally went back to pick up the bike.

Why did he pull over and puke?

I don't want to speak for Jason, but I have had many clients in very similar situations, and here is what I think is generally going on:

The only thing I can come up with—as extreme and ridiculous as it might sound to somebody—is to think of the person who beat you up, the person who shot you, the person who raped you, the person who hurt you the most. Now imagine having to go and buy them a gift. Not just any gift. The very thing that person wants. Imagine buying a gift for the person who has hurt you the most. Imagine buying a gift for the person you disdain the most in this world.

How hard would that be? You have to face that person in a way, and you must know them, and it's almost like you're saying they deserve the gift. And when that person is yourself, I believe it's the hardest of all.

I believe that that's the relationship that Jason had with himself.

People who judge themselves have such disdain and such overwhelming judgment toward themselves that the idea of looking after themselves and buying something for themselves literally sickens them to the core.

When he sent me a Facebook message picture of him with his little boy, driving down the road on the bike, you could feel it. It was such an iconic photograph, especially in the context of his life. He was bringing his boy with him and wasn't running from his family.

When he walked in the next weekend, everybody looked at him and went, "What the hell happened to you?"

He floated into the room. He was finally looking out for himself, to the degree that his wife was a bit concerned about all the positive changes.

This guy didn't believe he deserved anything. He thought

his sole function was to protect his family and give them everything they wanted, never what he needed.

But then he was freed up because of the story he shared with us.

Jason was sexually abused, and when I asked him to do a One Last Talk, that was the last thing he wanted to talk about. No one knew about it except him and the person who abused him. By the end, he decided to go on stage and share about the abuse.

That freed him from the past in a way he could never have imagined. He never thought that, by sharing what he was most ashamed of, he would be free in a way he could only dream about.

The first thing that happened for him was that he was able to better connect at home. He was able to allow himself permission to stay at home. He pivoted his business to become the father he never imagined he could be.

The second thing was that he was able to have very real conversations at home. He wasn't in great relationships and had been ignoring that. So he was able to step up and have some strong conversations at home.

Thirdly, he was able to process the resentment and

anger he held, which had a huge physical effect on him. He was overweight, and he lost over 30 pounds and kept it off.

He was also able to confront the cousin that abused him, and he created boundaries.

Before this, he had been running from it. He thought, *It happened. There's nothing I can do about it. I just need to move on.*

But he was completely oblivious to the effects it was having on his life.

When we're unaware of the cost, we just keep plowing and plowing through.

But we can't solve problems we refuse to acknowledge.

MITCH

Mitch was in a room with me, rambling about his business. He loves talking about business and is very comfortable with that conversation.

I looked at him and said, "How are things at home?"

He was offended by my rude interruption.

He said, "Yeah, things are good. My youngest child and I are struggling a bit, but that's it."

I said, "How are you struggling?"

He said, "He's doing a lot of the things that I did, and I feel like he's heading down a similar path. I try to help him, but I just get angry."

I asked, "What kinds of conversations are you having with him?"

He said, "It's interesting you say that. Last night, I sat him down, and we had a conversation."

"What was the conversation?" I asked.

He said, "I told him, 'If you could listen to me, you'd be better off.'"

The moment I heard that, I knew where this was going. I said, "How did that go down?"

He said, "Not great."

"Well, where had you heard that conversation before?" I asked.

He looked at me, paused, and said, "You bastard."

He doesn't usually get emotional, but he nodded his head and started tearing up.

"My dad," he said. "My God."

I said, "What would it be like to go to your boy, sit him down, look him in the eye, and say, 'I'm scared. I don't know what to do. I'm afraid of losing you. Tell me what you want me to do so I can get out of your way or be here for you.'?"

I looked at this man, and there was a stream of tears rolling down his face. These were the exact words he needed to hear from his own father. They were the words he desperately needed, yet he was repeating history all over again with this son.

This started Mitch on the path toward really engaging with his son. But it wasn't easy. Because of the baggage from their first fifteen years or so, his son was not eager to engage.

Mitch said to me once, "I really want my kid to go to One Last Talk. But I know he won't go."

"Why not?"

"Because if I were his age, I wouldn't have gone."

And I said, "Well, why don't you just say that to him?"

And he said, "What do you mean?"

"Just say something like: by the way, son, if my dad had asked me this when I was your age, I would say no to this. But I want you to just listen before you say no. Just maybe sit with it and think about it."

By admitting that he would have said no in his position, Mitch gave his son an insight into who he was when he was sixteen, and he was sharing with vulnerability.

And to Mitch's surprise, his son actually came back and said yes. They connected much deeper at One Last Talk, and then they ended up going to Peru together on a trip.

His son went from not wanting to spend a day with his dad in the city he lived in, to spending seven days in Peru, giving back to orphans, working with kids, and hiking in the mountains.

Mitch created this by digging into his past, seeing what was there, and then using it to connect to his son in the present.

SCOTT

Scott was a founder and CEO of a financial business. For his sixtieth birthday, he said, "I want to go to Ireland with you and your group." That was his gift to himself.

At BraveSoul, we go through the process of "past, present, and future." We ask every single question we can to mine the past. Then we create a bridge to the present and a bridge to the future. It's extraordinary how it all ties together.

We give people the option to share their stories. When we did this, the CEO said, "You know, I have a great past. My first memory was of getting a bicycle, and I had such freedom and independence. I know you expect some sad story, but my past was genuinely brilliant."

Eventually, people were joking with him in a respectful way, saying, "Here's Mr. Perfect," or "Here's Mr. Happy."

One night, we were in the bar, and he said to me, "If you don't mind me asking, is there something I'm missing about my past?"

I said, "I don't think that it's about missing something. I think you're too busy telling yourself a story of how great your past is that you don't have the opportunity to step back and wonder and dream about the possibility that it wasn't the way you've characterized it. You're also likely protecting your parents. You don't want to dare face a reality that maybe they didn't give you what you needed as a child."

I think that second point is true for anyone.

I love my dad. He's amazing. But he did shit to me that he didn't even realize and, at times, didn't give me what I needed when I was a kid.

Anyway, Scott walked in the following morning, and I didn't know who this guy was. The philanthropist, everything's-perfect, optimist guy was just gone.

He was angry. You could see it in his eyes. He said:

> *Can I just share something? I told you the other day that I had independence and joy and everything else in my past. Well, that's a lie. I was a fucking lonely kid, and I'm fucking mad that I was lonely. My parents did give me a bike, but I cycled around for days on end without any friends. I never realized I had so much anger and where that's affecting me today.*
>
> *Now I see the results in my business and life. I have an open-door policy at work. I let people come in and tell*

me whatever they want—as long as I agree with it. I'm a dictator, but a passive-aggressive one.

I tell myself I'm a philanthropist, a good guy, but I actually don't have a lot of connections. I'm not that connected to my kids or my wife. I'm not even that connected to myself. I was lonely then, and I'm lonely now.

All his life, he didn't want to see it.

He had never taken time to see how his past was affecting him.

These stories may seem simple, but a lot of work is required to get to the finished result.

Now they understand who they are and how to understand their past in a way that benefits them.

But they got there because they were willing to look at their past.

Here's the principle to remember as you do the next exercise: our future is contained within our past.

Our pasts create our futures, but our present choices can change our futures too.

3.5

Exercise: The 5 Days

THE 5 HAPPIEST DAYS

There are two tightly linked exercises that I use to help people go deeper after the One Last Message. I call it The 5 Days Exercise. We start by answering this question:

What have been the five happiest days in your life?

They don't have to be days when we were happy from nine o'clock in the morning to ten o'clock at night. It's more about identifying the instant—the moment that was pivotal that made the whole day so meaningful.

Once those days are identified—and this is crucial—for each one, you ask this question:

What was it that made that day so happy for you?

The full exercise is to identify the days, rank them, and then think about why these days were so special.

After doing the exercise with my wife, she said her number one happiest day was our wedding day. Mine was my bachelor's party.

It wasn't because we went off and got drunk. We did the opposite. My friends and I did a workshop and hiked through the mountains in County Clare, Ireland, and I remember seeing people experience breakthroughs.

The point of the exercise is simple: to identify those moments in life that were our happiest and impacted us in significant ways.

[You can fill this out online here: https://onelasttalk.com/book.]

What have been the five happiest days in your life?

Happiest Day 1:

Q: What was it that made that day so happy for you?

Happiest Day 2:

Q: What was it that made that day so happy for you?

Happiest Day 3:

Q: What was it that made that day so happy for you?

Happiest Day 4:

Q: What was it that made that day so happy for you?

Happiest Day 5:

Q: What was it that made that day so happy for you?

The point of this exercise is that aligning with joy is important. Everything doesn't have to be darkness.

THE 5 DARKEST DAYS

For a lot of people, it's hard to come up with their five best days. I've heard people say, "I struggled with coming up with five happiest days. But if you'd ask me to identify the darkest days of my life, I'd be asking for more paper."

The 5 Darkest Days exercise works the same way as the happiest days. It's about identifying the days that have held the greatest darkness for you.

To know whether you're doing this exercise correctly, you should notice some sort of visceral reaction. Your heart's pounding, you've got a knot in your stomach, you're getting angry, or you feel like burning the paper and throwing it in the garbage.

In short, you're irritated and probably don't want to do the exercise. You're pissed off and think it's stupid. You judge the exercise because it's stirring you.

We've found that this exercise helps people gain inspiration for their One Last Talk.

This exercise is about self-awareness. A lot of people want

to focus on the positive side and put the best stuff about their lives on Facebook, but they struggle with facing the reality that they've experienced a lot of pain, and they hope it will just go away.

But it won't. The question they should face instead is this:

How do your darkest days affect you today? And what is one thing you could do to move through it or beyond it? Or even just accept it?

It's not one of the cool exercises, telling people that we're going to focus on their five darkest days. But in the context of your One Last Talk, it helps identify and provide a framework for your experiences.

[Or, you can fill this out online here: https://onelasttalk. com/book.]

What have been the five darkest days in your life?

Darkest Day 1:

Q: What was it that made that day so bad for you?

Darkest Day 2:

Q: What was it that made that day so bad for you?

Darkest Day 3:

Q: What was it that made that day so bad for you?

Darkest Day 4:

Q: What was it that made that day so bad for you?

Darkest Day 5:

Q: What was it that made that day so bad for you?

3.6

Living in Your Head vs. Living in Your Truth

The One Last Talk exercises are designed to help people get out of their heads on a very basic level.

I don't think people realize how heady they are. We're spending so much time thinking. We think meditation or yoga or more information are the answers—that they will draw us out of our heads.

I'm not saying they can't help, but that's not what One Last Talk is about.

I think a lot of people actually use meditation to mask their truth. I did a meditation retreat once. I was intrigued, but meditation never fully landed for me. And that pissed me off.

The leader was a lovely lady, and I connected with her. I remember her saying, "Meditation saved my life."

I said, "What do you mean by that?"

She said, "I've been in the TV production world, and there's so much pressure there. Meditation keeps me sane to some extent. It keeps me grounded."

Do you see that?

The problem—her job and the pressure from it—is still there. She's not addressing the reasons her job is so stressful and why she still stays in it.

The problem is that she's out of alignment. Either she's in the wrong profession or she's orienting to her profession in the wrong way.

She's using meditation to hide the core issue—her job—and not address it.

I think meditation and yoga can aid and enhance our journey on this earth, and they can be great for some people. But I don't see them as the answers. They are tools to help find the answers, but not the answers themselves.

(And yes, One Last Talk is the exact same thing: a tool to help you find answers. It is not the answer.)

I was at dinner once with some friends, and a woman said something really interesting. She was giving advice to another person about raising kids, and she said, "It will all be over like that, and they'll be gone."

The other woman said, "I don't find that. I find that it has gone really slowly."

I tend to agree. I find that time passes by quickly when you aren't connected. I think this is because life just whizzes past when you're living in your head. But when you are connected, time passes slower.

This is what I mean:

People are pissed off and distracted. They're worried about their age. They don't like their name. They don't like themselves. And they just feel like they're just pissing their lives away. They're not using their lives. They are just going about the motions.

When they finally connect, ten years have already passed, and they don't know what just happened.

When you aren't living in your head, you're feeling your way through life instead of thinking your way through it.

That's the difference.

Connected people—people living in their soul and their truth—*feel* their way through life.

I'm not talking about some fluffy nonsense like, "Oh, everything will be great. This book will just write itself, and I'll sit back and manifest it into existence with my emotions."

In fact, that's the problem: people believe that feeling is like little doves landing on your shoulder with a message in their claw. It will be rolled out for you, and then you can just go get a cup of tea and be great.

That's not how it works.

Emotions can be hard.

Feeling can be painful at times.

If you think emotions are too hard to deal with, it's probably because you don't experience them. People who have the hardest time with emotions are almost always the ones pushing them away, because they are frightened by them.

How often you visit your emotions will determine how hard it is to deal with them.

For very heady people who go through the One Last Talk process, it feels like they are cutting their heart out and serving it up on a plate.

One of the most important things in life is asking the question, "What do I need to let go of first? What do I need to let go of that I'm holding on to?"

That is a key part of living in your truth, and part of what One Last Talk is designed to help people do.

In reality, when you get out of your head, you start to connect and don't need to control anymore. You let go of the need to control and move into life and feeling.

Another story explains this concept well. I call it my 9.75 story.

I was chatting with a girl who wanted some coaching with me, and she had filled out a questionnaire beforehand. For happiness, on a scale of one to 10, she said hers was 9.75.

So, I got on the phone with her and I said, "Great. Before we start, when's your coaching program starting?"

She said, "What are you talking about?"

I said, "Your coaching program."

She said, "I'm not a coach."

I said, "Oh, just curious, because I was going to sign up. You said your happiness was at 9.75. I want a bit of that. I want to know how you're so incredibly happy. Assuming of course it's true."

Yes, before you say it—I know I was being a bit of a dick, coming out guns blazing like that. But with her, I just felt it would work. I've never done this once, in my entire life, except with her.

We kept talking, and she insisted she was that happy. So eventually, I had her describe all the things she does, and I started filling the page.

Eventually, the page was completely full. It looked like I spilled a bottle of ink on it.

I said, "Anything else?"

She said, "No, I think that covers it."

I said, "There is no way on earth—it is not even remotely

possible—that you were a 9.75. It is not remotely possible. You cannot be doing all of this stuff and be happy. What am I not seeing?"

She said, "Okay, I had a bout of serious depression two years ago. But I'm past that now. I'm happy."

I went, "Ahhh. Let me explain something that may or may not align for you. You were in the depths of the darkness. It was so dark you never imagined you'd even come out of it. You crawled your way up to a baseline of zero. You popped your head up, and you felt a tiny bit of happiness. But for you, because your baseline was so low, it feels like you climbed to 9.75. What you really are is 0.75."

She was treading water, and she was pouring so much stuff into her life because she was afraid to create a space where she might slip back into depression. [If you're curious, I don't know what happened with her, because she never worked with me.]

One of the biggest fears for people who suffer depression is that, if they're not super busy every minute of the day, they might stop to feel their emotions, and they fear they're going to go backwards.

I know so many people who are just constantly doing stuff. If they have a moment of space in their life, they fill it with 50 things. They do this because, if they stop, the negative emotions will start to come up. They feel it. So, it's like they're running constantly, but they're running from their shadow.

One Last Talk is a way to get at that. Instead of running from whatever it is you're running from, you're actually turning directly into it.

One of my favorite psychological studies, and this has been replicated again and again and again,* is that when you give people a choice between sitting in a room alone for five minutes and painful electric shocks, they would actually rather take the shocks.

Think about that: *most people would rather take painful electric shocks than be alone with their thoughts and feelings.*

This is the essence of "living in your head," and people who live in their heads are doing so because they feel that they're safe in there. That if they're in their head they don't have to feel.

But feeling is where the work is done, and feeling is where the truth is, and feeling is how you move past the pain.

---

* Timothy D. Wilson, David A. Reinhard, Erin C. Westgate, Daniel T. Gilbert, Nicole Ellerbeck, Cheryl Hahn, Casey L. Brown, Adi Shaked. See all authors and affiliations. See also, Science 04 Jul 2014: Vol. 345, Issue 6192, pp. 75–77, DOI: 10.1126/science.1250830.

And One Last Talk is a way to help you feel what you have been avoiding.

3.7

Exercise: The Ten-Year-Old in the Picture

This is an exercise that we use a lot to break people open who are having problems getting deep and real with themselves.

Here are the instructions:

Get a photograph of your ten-year-old self.

Stare at it for 15 minutes.

Feel everything that comes up.

Ask yourself, "What are the words I really needed to hear at that age?"

Then write down the words you needed to hear.

[You can do this here as well: https://onelasttalk.com/book.]

It's important that you find it as close as possible to the age of ten. Seven or eight or nine will work, but not much above ten, because once you get into the teenage years, it brings you to a different place.

Ten is pre-puberty, and I think pre-puberty is more grounded. People can connect with a more innocent version of themselves, not influenced by external factors like trying to fit in. I find that around ten years old brings you to a rawer emotional place.

It's not about how to set goals, dream big, whatever. It's not "use 10 percent of your income and do this" or "buy Bitcoin in 2011" or any nonsense like that.

Your advice to your ten-year-old self will be the words you needed to hear yourself. It's leading you to a compassionate place.

When you stare at that picture, don't be shocked at the incredible judgment and harshness that comes out of you initially.

Then, when you get into the emotions, don't be shocked to find that compassion and acceptance come out.

This is why it's so important for some people to start with the photograph first. You have to connect with the emotion that the ten-year-old was feeling at that time.

What was that kid feeling? What was that kid saying? What did that kid want to say?

Once you do that, stuff is going to come out.

But that doesn't happen unless you connect with how that kid was feeling.

It's not just writing a letter to the ten-year-old kid.

It's writing based on how they were feeling at the time and what they needed to hear.

3.8

Moving from Judgment to Compassion

When we ask people to look at the picture of their ten-year-old selves for 15 minutes, they often go through a rollercoaster of emotions.

Initially, it's awkward.

I'm sitting in a room and staring at a photograph of myself. This is so weird.

Then, typically, they go to a place of judgment of their ten-year-old self.

Here's a story that illustrates this:

I did a workshop years ago in Toronto, and there was a guy in it who was not engaged. He was looking at the wall, looking out the window, picking his nails. I asked him, "What's going on?"

He said, "Nothing, I'm here."

I said, "No, you're not. You weren't here yesterday, and you aren't here today. What's going on? It's fine if you're not here. I just want to see what's going on."

He said, "No, I'm getting it. Where do I start?"

"I don't know. It's your life. Tell me about now."

He said, "My biggest challenge is that I start stuff and don't finish."

"Okay. What's that about?"

He said, "I don't know. I thought you might have the answer."

I said, "I don't have the answer, but the answer is not on the wall or out the window, I know that."

He said, "Okay. Why do I start things and not finish them?"

"I don't know. Tell me about your life."

He said, "I grew up in Toronto—a black kid in a white neighborhood. You know the deal."

"I'm a white Irishman, and I didn't grow up in Toronto. I don't know the deal. Tell me what the deal was."

"It was hard," he said.

"How was it hard?" I asked.

He answered with a tone that expressed a lot of anger. Especially toward himself. So, I went into that.

"What exactly makes you so angry at yourself?" I asked.

"There were days where I would put white powder on my face to try to fit in."

And I said, "Wednesdays?"

"What do you mean?" he said.

I said, "Just on a Wednesday?"

He said, "No, every day."

"For how long?" I asked.

"Probably three or four years," he said.

At this point, I was barely holding back the tears. Probably everyone in the room was crying, and yet he had this stern, judgmental face on.

I pulled a chair into the middle of the room and said, "Your ten-year-old self is sitting there with the white powder on his face. What would you say to him?"

He blurted out, "Grow a fucking set of balls. Don't be so fucking weak. Don't be such a fucking loser."

I said, "There, my friend, is the single biggest challenge you have. You have such a disdain for who you have been and, therefore, who you are today. Your journey, if you choose to take it, is to be able to sit in front of that chair someday and look at that kid and say, 'You know what, buddy? You did your best. You don't need to wear the white stuff on your face, but I understand why you did it.' You have to be able to have compassion and self-love for that boy. Until you do that, it's never going to be enough, because you're not enough. You'll find any way to validate your negative feelings about yourself until that happens."

People go through judgment until they find a little gap of

compassion. If they drop into that compassion, stuff will open up. They will accept that little kid in a way they've never done before.

The usual pattern is: weirdness, then judgment, then compassion, and then, hopefully, acceptance.

But sometimes people don't ever come out of judgment. They find it hard to get out of that place. It's the first time they've tried, and there's so much self-judgment.

Most people don't like who they are.

They'll say they do, but they don't.

They'll talk about self-love but ignore how much judgment they have about their bodies, their businesses, their relationships, their regrets—whatever it is that haunts them.

But that's okay. For many people, it's part of the process to recognize that you are judging yourself so harshly.

It's also part of the process to move past that.

And then you move into acceptance, and then self-love.

If you find yourself overwhelmed with judgment while

looking at the picture, stop the exercise. Take a break and come back to it.

The next time, consider what it would be like to be softer and more gentle. It's as simple as that. Literally ask yourself:

What would it look like if I were kind to myself?

What if I liked that kid? What would change then?

It's very simple, but I've seen this blow people open.

But there's a lot of judgment toward the exercise itself. You saw it in the example above.

If I'm 40 years old, what the hell am I doing looking at a photograph of myself when I was a kid? This is ridiculous.

I think compassion is a natural gateway to acceptance. Within compassion is also understanding.

In the story of the guy who hated his younger self, he had to get to that point of saying, "What were you doing, you fucking loser?" to really begin understanding and connecting with why he was feeling this way.

Compassion is the gateway, and it can be very brief, like

an elevator you're in. Then you say, "Oh, that's why I did what I did."

In a sense, understanding can be the bridge between judgment and compassion.

It's not just intellectual understanding, but really connecting to the feelings of what made you do what you did at that age that moves you from judgment to compassion.

(You might be asking what him starting and not finishing anything has to do with putting white powder on his face when he was ten years old.

I can explain pretty easily: it's self-sabotage.

When you hate yourself, you don't feel you deserve success, and you will—unconsciously—make sure you don't achieve it.

This guy was successful, but he had all kinds of opportunities in front of him to do much more and either would not take them, found some excuse, or screwed up these opportunities so that he did not have to accomplish them.)

3.9

One Last Letter Explanation & Prompts

WHAT IS A ONE LAST LETTER?

The One Last Letter is the next step in the One Last Talk process. It's where you sit down and write out the theoretical "last letter" you will ever write. The letter you want to leave behind. This becomes the basis for your One Last Talk.

The instructions for your One Last Letter are very simple, just like your One Last Message:

> *In one or two pages, what's the One Last Letter you'd want to write before you left this planet, and who would you write it to? Take no more than 15 minutes to write this, and make sure you write it to a specific person.*

You might feel ready; however, I would recommend you read this chapter before starting the exercise in the next chapter.

SOME EXAMPLES OF ONE LAST LETTERS

Remember the guidelines for One Last Talk:

- You must speak YOUR truth in the speech.
- Your talk must be based on your personal experience and your feelings only.
- No prescriptive elements (e.g., "Here are four easy steps to change...").
- No advice (e.g., "You need to do this...").
- No preaching or moralizing (e.g., "You should feel this way...").
- No virtue signaling (e.g., "Look at these schools I built in Cambodia...").
- You must deliver the talk to at least ONE other human (in person, if at all possible).

I bring these up because I'm going to show you two examples of real One Last Letters. One of them follows these guidelines, and one does not.

I'm showing you both examples because I want you to see what the differences between them look like and read like. You'll see and feel the difference between when someone actually digs deep, addresses a specific person, and faces their truth, versus when they turn away by offering advice or telling others what to do.

I want to emphasize that the one that doesn't follow the guidelines isn't "wrong." It's just early in the evolution of someone uncovering their truth, and that's okay. Sometimes you have to start there to get deeper.

ONE LAST LETTER #1, FOLLOWS GUIDELINES

Dad,

Several years ago, I wrote you a letter that today I am not proud of. In fact, the thought of it leads me to believe it was from another lifetime. We were both vastly different people compared to whom we are now, both individually and as father/son.

I'm writing you this letter to let you know how proud I am to call you my dad. Neither of us knows when our last day will be. I would be heartbroken if I left things unsaid.

You and I haven't always aligned or connected over the years, but let's be honest—what father and son do? I've come to appreciate that all of our experiences together, good-bad-indifferent, have simply been a part of the journey that has shaped who we both are today. I'm incredibly proud of who we both are and how these experiences have shaped the relationship we have today. Although I'm not proud of how I've handled every moment, I wouldn't change a thing.

Remember the bike I crashed in 2010? Yeah, I didn't get hit by a car and fall into a ditch. I was a jackass and entered a wet corner too fast and dropped the bike. But you know that. Over the years, I've found myself embellishing the truth to you on trivial things that don't matter. I'm not exactly sure why. Likely in a sincere attempt to get your respect, your attention, and to feel seen. Even still, to this day.

I'm sorry for not always seeking to understand your point of view and experience over the years. I feel like I've left you out to dry and haven't been there to support you or have your back during difficult times, whether it was during your divorce with mom, grandpa passing, or simple challenges of every day. I've come to peace with this, but I need you to know that I've reflected on this and wish I had handled these moments differently.

This past month, I spent a great deal of time thinking about you, both in Canada and Colorado. A very important and difficult question came up for me.

Am I happy with our relationship? And do I wish to deepen it?

My honest answer? I'm happy with where our relationship has come to, but I'd like to deepen it and spend more time together. It's awkward and a bit strange for me, because I don't know what that looks like or where to exactly start. But I'd like to spend more time with you, and that's important to me.

So it's difficult for me to ask. Are you happy with our relationship? Are you interested in deepening it?

I love you. Thank you for everything you've done for me and continue to do.

Dave

ONE LAST LETTER #2, DOES NOT FOLLOW GUIDELINES

Dear Everyone and Anyone,

These are the last words you will ever hear from me, and yet these will be the most important words you will ever read.

As you travel the long and winding road of life, know that you will meet several challenges along the way. You will find a path that is sometimes very straight and the direction is clear, and at other times you will not be able to see what's up ahead.

You are to press on, trusting that what lies just around the bend is the true magnificence of your life. You are not to give up, as there is nothing along this journey you cannot overcome.

There will be others of you whose road is met with steep hills and bumps—again, you are not to turn back, for some of the greatest gifts of life await you at the top of the hills or along those bumpy roads.

Still others will find their roads crowded with lots of traffic, surrounded by distraction, deafened by sounds and noise of life. You too are not to give up, for the magic is found in the silence and stillness of your life.

You might ask how I know this to be true. My answer is simple: I have traveled all these roads a million times; I have endured and overcome not just physical and emotional abuse from others, but even worse from myself; I used to allow the uncertainty and unfairness of life make me a victim who refused to even get on the road of life; I used to blame others for my not being able to see the path that was right in front of me; I used to give up at what seemed to be insurmountable challenges that kept me from my dreams; I allowed the noise of society and the voices of others to define my path.

Until one day, I stopped searching and looking for the answers outside of myself.

They had been there all along on my path—my road to my dreams and everything I ever wanted had already been given to me. For my road was built on the inside, the straight part of the road already built on confidence and creativity. The uncertain hills and valleys paved by faith and belief in myself. The challenges and distractions on the next part of my road easily handled by focus and determination.

You see, no matter what your road looks like, the only block in the road is you. There is nothing and no one who can stop you the minute you decide.

So decide to build the road that makes you happy—the road that allows you to show your brilliance that is lit up by the joy and happiness you bring to the world. Stop looking outside, for the answer is a thought and belief away.

WHY DO A ONE LAST LETTER? CAN'T I JUST GO STRAIGHT TO ONE LAST TALK?

You should do the One Last Letter before a One Last Talk because it allows you to get to a deeper place when it comes to your truth.

We're in a society where we're always looking for shortcuts. We don't want the results today; we want them yesterday.

For example, I just moved into a new house. I asked the painter, "Do you really have to prime the wall before painting?"

He said, "No. But do you want me to do it right?"

We're looking for quick fixes. We want to get to the outcome without going through the process, but that's the point people are not getting—*the process is how you get the result.*

In fact, that is why I showed you One Last Letters that "break" the rules of One Last Talk. To show you that this is an evolution, and it does not come out perfectly right away.

HOW TO WRITE YOUR ONE LAST LETTER

People ask, "Who am I writing to?"

I say, "Whoever you want to. It's your letter. Write it to anyone you'd like. Family, friends, yourself at a younger age. It's up to you—just make it an actual person."

People ask, "What do I say?"

I answer, "Whatever you feel you need to say. To whomever you need to say it."

I might give readers some questions to ask themselves

to inspire the answer, but it's not ABC or multiple choice. (Note: if you are really having trouble coming up with something, there are prompts later on in this chapter)

The letter should move someone emotionally. Specifically, you.

This is an exercise to draw you out of your head—to connect you emotionally with your truth and what you're feeling.

When you write your one last letter, you need to be emotionally connected. There's no magic to it.

When you're connected with your emotions, you can speak more about your truth. It will just flow.

HOW NOT TO WRITE YOUR ONE LAST LETTER

Even though there is not a "right" way to do it, there are a few ways that don't help you. You read the examples already, so you saw what happens when it goes wrong. If you want to get it right, avoid these things:

Don't rush through it. Take the time you need.

Don't do it for the sake of doing it. Dig in emotionally.

Don't do it if you've not bought in.

Don't come at from a very intellectual, heady place. Connect with your emotions.

Don't try to be clever. Be direct.

Don't try to frame it perfectly. Just put it out there.

Don't focus on the grammar and the words you use. Focus on the message.

Don't spend the letter telling others what to do and giving advice. Focus on you and what you feel and need to do.

If the letter is something you would immediately be proud to share with the whole world, you're probably not going deep enough. If that's the case, your motivation is about looking good.

HOW DO I KNOW IF I'M DOING IT RIGHT?

There is no right or perfect One Last Talk, One Last Message, or One Last Letter.

Do not self-judge the letter. That's not what this is about. It's not about the letter not being good enough or being right.

If you find yourself crying, feeling, and connected to your

emotions, that indicates you're in the right frame of being. Sit with that; stay with it. That means you're doing it right.

If you find yourself very heady and overthinking it, take a break from it. Go for a walk. Just get away from it for a little while and create some space. Let your emotions come back into the process.

What you have to understand is that a mix of emotions is a good thing.

People say, "My God, I got really angry. What the hell is wrong with me?"

Nothing is wrong with you. You're human. You feel emotion.

You should be feeling whatever emotions are there: anger, frustration, joy. You might even need a box of Kleenex because you're bawling.

If you are judging yourself, what you're writing, and the words you're using, that's okay. That's part of the process.

Don't write based on whether or not your wife will open up the book and read it. Write the letter you know you need to write in your soul.

It's not about coming from a place of knowing it all. It's not lecturing. That's what your dad did to you—finger pointing, saying "If you could just listen to me."

The minute you go there, you're telling instead of feeling, and you're not connecting with the other person.

It's an exercise to open up the heart. There aren't a lot of instructions around it beyond the simple ones.

PROMPTS YOU CAN USE

If the previous exercises and prompts haven't been enough to really help you figure out your One Last Letter topic, then try these. If any of them connect, then use them:

What's the hardest thing you've ever had to face in your life?

Was there ever a time you felt like on paper you were successful, yet inside you felt like a failure?

What's the one thing that has kept you awake more nights than anything else?

What is the absolute darkest depth of despair you've ever felt?

Have you ever been pushed too far? Who pushed you?

Is there something in your past that you're ashamed of?

Is there something you've never shared with anyone else, even your closest loved ones?

What cost have you paid for not following your dreams?

Was there ever a time in your life when you felt alone, or as though nobody understood you?

Is there something you're holding onto a tremendous amount of guilt about?

What changes have you made that have resulted in a more fulfilling life?

What one thing makes you the most proud of yourself?

What's the one conversation that you need to have with someone but are afraid to?

3.10

Exercise: Write Your One Last Letter

Ok, now that I've explained it, it's time to sit down and actually write your One Last Letter.

The instructions for your One Last Letter are very simple, just like your One Last Message:

> In one or two pages, write the One Last Letter you'd want to write before you left this planet. Take no more than fifteen minutes to write this, and make sure you write it to a specific person.

[You can also fill this out here: https://onelasttalk.com/book.]

PART

DELIVER
YOUR TRUTH

FOUR

Before You Write
Your One Last Talk

Just to refresh, here are the One Last Talk instructions and rules:

> *If you had One Last Talk to give before you left this planet, what would you say, and who would you say it to?*

SPEAKER RULES

- Fifteen minutes (or less).
- No slides or visuals.
- You must speak YOUR truth in the speech.
- Your talk must be based on your personal experience and your feelings only.

- No prescriptive elements (e.g., "Here are four easy steps to change...").
- No advice (e.g., "You need to do this...").
- No preaching or moralizing (e.g., "You should feel this way...").
- No virtue signaling (e.g., "Look at these schools I built in Cambodia...").
- You must deliver the talk to at least ONE other human (in person, if at all possible).

LISTENER RULES

- No interruptions.
- No judgment.
- No questions.
- When the talk is finished, tell the speaker what you are going to do differently in your life because of what you heard in the talk.

That's it.

YOUR ONE LAST TALK IS NOT ABOUT TRAINING

I know some of the best storytellers and speakers in the world. I could bring them in and have them write thousands of pages and describe in excruciating detail exactly how to craft a perfect story and talk.

And not one bit of that will actually help you with your One Last Talk.

Because your resistance (if you have any) is not about how to craft a talk. Your resistance is about other things.

One Last Talk is not about speaker training. It's not about storytelling.

It is only about connecting with yourself and your pain and your truth, then sharing that truth openly with people.

YES, 15 MINUTES IS ENOUGH TIME

We have specific timing for the talks, and some people say, "How can I tell this in less than 15 minutes?" You hear that number and think, *Oh, that's a quick coffee.*

But 15 minutes is a fucking lifetime on a stage. It's like two hours in real life.

The first time I did a short talk, it was seven minutes, and I was astonished at what I could cover. It was challenging, but it was also rewarding. It was probably one of the best talks I've ever done. I loved the fact that I had to condense it into seven minutes.

NO, YOU DON'T NEED SLIDES

I think slides allow you to move out of yourself and away from connecting.

It's a crutch. People ask if they can use just one slide, and I say no. No slides. No handouts.

REMINDER: IT MUST BE PERSONAL

Remember Bev's original desire to talk about the First Nations or Brian's original desire to talk about the Five Fs?

Bev's could have been a very moving story, and Brian's would have been impactful intellectually. But neither works as a One Last Talk because neither is personal.

You have to use your personal story to make it a One Last Talk. It's non-negotiable that the story must be personal. It's never about an idea; it's always personal.

A One Last Talk cannot be a story about something that lies outside of you. It's a story that matters to you.

One Last Talk could be compared to TED, but for human connection. Most TED Talks could be delivered by anybody with the same platform, because the talk is about "ideas worth spreading."

That's not true with a One Last Talk.

Your talk can't be delivered by anyone else.

It's personal, and it's yours alone.

REMINDER: NO COACHING, NO ADVISING, NO PREACHING

Some people want to turn a question to the audience and go into coaching mode. They want to coach the world—they want to tell you what to do and lecture you.

Coaching, advising, and preaching should not be part of a One Last Talk.

Your One Last Talk MUST be focused on your truth and your pain and what you might do differently, and perhaps what you might do differently in the future. But not on anyone else.

So if you're telling people what they need to do, it's not a One Last Talk.

If you're telling people how screwed up their political system or their religious system is, it's not a One Last Talk.

If you're just expressing your anger toward somebody who has victimized you, that's not a One Last Talk.

If you find yourself wanting to present yourself like a heroic character, it's not your One Last Talk.

If your talk portrays you as having all the answers, it's not a One Last Talk.

If you find yourself wanting to change the story to protect people and to soften the blow, you're not going deep enough, and that's not a One Last Talk.

It's not that you have to name names, but you do have to face the reality. You're probably very concerned about what others are going to think of the truth, and there's a strong likelihood that you're manipulating the truth to counter that. In this case, the One Last Talk will lack depth.

The minute you shift your finger toward the audience, the energy is gone. It's dead.

People will think, *Here we go again. Another person telling me how I should live my life.*

They don't even know what happened; they can just feel it.

Think about this in relation to Bev's speech. She didn't say, "Here's what you should do with your kids."

Instead, she said, "If I could turn back the clock, this is what I would have done."

Of everything we've covered, *this is the most pivotal aspect of One Last Talk.*

In our culture, preaching is so connected to hypocrisy. Like the anti-homosexual politicians who are secretly gay, or the celebrities who fly in their private jets to preach to poor people about being better to the environment.

People who preach at you are implicitly telling you they are better than you.

I'm not saying everyone who lectures is a hypocrite. I think a lot of people have a genuine desire to help others. But if all you want to do is tell others what to do, you're escaping from feeling rather than connecting with your feelings on a very basic, human level.

The minute you say, "If you ever find yourself in that situation, here is what you should do," is the minute you start trying to escape the feeling. You're trying to escape the vulnerability. You don't want to connect with it because you don't know what to do with it.

For most people, if it doesn't have an intellectual purpose, they don't know what to do with it.

When you make it about you and your pain and your truth, and that's it, you have skin in the game.

Now people will listen, and they'll let it impact them.

4.2

Outline Your One
Last Talk

If you're here, it means you've uncovered your truth, and now you want to start to get it down on paper and give your actual talk.

At this point, some people ask, "How do I do it? Where do I start? Where do I finish? What do I do?"

First off, relax. We have a framework for your One Last Talk that you can use if you need it.

The first thing I'm going to tell you is very simple: *the framework below is NOT required*.

It's not even necessarily recommended. It is just a simple, effective framework that helps ease people's nerves.

A lot of people begin with our structure, and they eventually realize they don't need it and use a different one, which is fine.

Do not feel wedded to it at all. Use it, change it, discard it, whatever you want. If you look back at all the One Last Talks that we have shared, not even half follow this format.

That's totally fine.

And most importantly, do not think your One Last Talk has to follow the conventional boom-bust-boom format, or the hero's journey, or any story form you've heard about.

All that matters is that you actually uncover your truth and then speak it to someone.

Whatever format you use that does that, it's right.

We teach a unique framework. Instead of trying to create rules about storytelling, we just outline the five common parts of many One Last Talks, then we explain them in the order they tend to occur in most One Last Talks. That's it.

The five commonly recurring elements of One Last Talks are:

- Part 1: Start in the Moment
- Part 2: Give Necessary Backstory
- Part 3: What Changed (or Woke You Up)?
- Part 4: What Happened Because of That Change?
- Part 5: Where Are You Now?

[If you'd like to outline your One Last Talk in our template, you can go to the site and do it there, https://onelasttalk. com/book.]

I'll explain very briefly what each part is and then give examples of each from actual One Last Talks.

PART 1: START IN THE MOMENT

It's important that when you walk out, you're able to get into it straight away. You jump right to the hard part.

My invitation is always to start your One Last Talk in that most emotionally intense moment.

Relive the moment in the midst of viscerally connecting to the pain. That's a really uncomfortable feeling, but it creates an incredible impact.

Or relive the happiness. Or the hardest moment. Whatever most stands out to you as the most emotionally intense, try to start there, actually describing it.

Example 1: Neely literally begins by talking about being sexually assaulted by her cousin and starts her One Last Talk detailing what was going through her mind.

Example 2: Quan begins with what seems like a very simple statement of fact, but it is deeply intense: he admits to committing a murder. That is the painful truth that Quan was running from for so long, and he starts right in it.

Example 3: You don't have to start with something painful. Rob Friend begins with a moment of intense joy, about to run onto the soccer pitch.

The point with each of these is that they begin in the moment of their truth—the assault, the murder, or the game. They are all "the moment" for that One Last Talk.

It's an invitation, because it's not a golden rule. For example, Bev's talk did not start in the moment. Instead, she gave backstory and built to the moment. That can also work.

PART 2: GIVE NECESSARY BACKSTORY

You only have 15 minutes, so giving extensive backstory is

usually not possible. Also, most people want to give lots of unnecessary backstory as a way of avoiding the actual intense parts of the speech.

Try to give the minimum amount of backstory necessary so that your audience can understand what's going on. That's it. This is not about rehashing history; this is about connecting with the emotion of your truth, so you want to spend as much time as possible talking about what changed and what happened for you after the change. That's the meat of the talk.

PART 3: WHAT CHANGED (OR WOKE YOU UP)?

This is the meat of the talk. Once you've given your backstory, what changed to shift you out of that? Did something happen to wake you up? Was it the emotional event that you led with? Did someone say something that shocked you out of your slumber?

It could be any number of things. What matters is that you dig into what precisely happened that diverted you off the path you were on and onto a new path.

And what exactly changed? Go deep into explaining the actual change that occurred. It is very important that you not skip over this. You must really dive in and be specific about what exactly changed for you.

Example 1: In Bev's talk, the thing that woke her up was her son's suicide. That was the thing that changed her whole world.

Example 2: For Quan, the wakeup call was that moment he realized his mind could be free—that he could see the world the way he wanted, even if his body was in prison.

Example 3: For Brian, the wakeup call was the second girl who had an abortion.

PART 4: WHAT HAPPENED BECAUSE OF THAT CHANGE?

Once you talk about the change itself, now you can talk about the impact it had on you and all the ripple effects through your life.

You should be answering questions like, what is the lesson you learned? What would your life be like had you never learned that lesson? What is your life like now?

Here are just a handful of personal details you might care to share with the audience to give them an update on your life:

- Relationship status updates.
- New pleasures you experience.
- New beliefs you hold.

- Physical transformations you've undergone.
- Mental clarity you now have.
- Personal growth you've experienced.
- Financial or career successes you've achieved.
- New aligned endeavors you've embarked upon.

It can be any of those things, or something else, but dig into what is actually different for you.

Example 1: For Donna, this looked like her being honest with herself and her girls, and then changing her life.

Example 2: For Matthew, this was about realizing that he was going to dive into life and engage it fully.

Example 3: For Bev, this was engaging her other son and being with him the way she had not been there for her first son.

PART 5: WHERE ARE YOU NOW?

This is about where you are now. After all this change, what are you doing differently? How do you see the world differently?

Remember, this is not about lecturing. It's about sharing what your experience and changes have left you with, and what it means for you personally going forward.

4.3

Write Your Talk

This step is optional. If you have outlined your talk, you are ready to give it. You do NOT have to write your talk fully out.

If you choose to write your talk out fully, that's okay as well. I have had One Last Talk speakers at the events do both, and either method can work.

The one thing I would recommend is that you NOT try to memorize the talk. This is not about delivering a perfect speech. This is about connecting with your emotions and your pain and your truth, and then speaking that out loud.

What I have seen work well for lots of speakers is outlining the talk, then writing it out, then just taking a list of the bullet points of the speech to help keep on track during the speech.

[If you'd like to write your speech out, you can go here to do it on our site: https://onelasttalk.com/book.]

Prepare to Give Your Talk

Now you have your talk outlined, and possibly even fully written out.

This is where we get into the scary work: the talk itself.

I would like to make this invitation:

Below are some suggestions to help you become more comfortable with your story. Go through them and choose which ones work for you.

HOW MUCH SHOULD I PREPARE?

I hear this question all the time. My attitude is that I don't over-prepare.

The more you prepare, the less connection you're going

to have to the truth, and that will affect you when you're in front of someone.

Remember that, when it comes to a vulnerable truth, you don't want to share it 20 times. If you do, you'll end up with a lifeless, mundane delivery. You become numb. I specifically tell people not to over-prepare for this reason.

Sure, run through a few times, and that's it. Then leave it alone. Maybe address it again a couple days before you deliver it in front of others, but that's it.

(It's basically the opposite of the TED structure. With that, you'd want to go over it 50 times, record it, and prepare it down to every minute detail.)

The most important point about preparing for One Last Talk is to not over-prepare. Over-preparing is delivering it multiple times in advance. I don't think you should record yourself, either, because everyone is too self-critical. That would be a mistake.

MEMORIZE THE TALK OR NOT?

I think you should know what you want to talk about, but you shouldn't memorize the words in between. You should know what the base is—the bullet points. If you do more than that, the audience can tell from a mile away.

A guy named Kenton Ho gave a talk in Toronto, and it was phenomenal, like he had been speaking his whole life.

But he'd never spoken before. He just moved and transitioned beautifully. You could tell he was ready, but it wasn't like, "Oh, I've nailed this sucker and know it all." He just knew what he needed to share.

He memorized the first line and spoke from the heart, so it was easy for him.

That's the whole idea.

NERVES

It's very common to be holding onto questions: "Is my truth enough? Is it good enough? Am I good enough? Can I deliver this?"

At this point, you might still face these questions.

There's nothing we can do to get you over them.

I say to people, "You feel nervous. I can help you a little, but I can't take away all the nerves. Which is fine, because it wouldn't be real if you didn't have any nerves."

A speaker who never gets nervous—it doesn't matter

who they are—is saying the same thing over and over and doesn't connect with it emotionally. Nothing is new. There's no vulnerability. It's over-rehearsed.

I'm not saying there's no value in that; it's just not what a One Last Talk is.

One Last Talk is about vulnerability, rawness, and connecting the pain and emotion and truth.

When you over-rehearse, you go to your head and away from your emotions. You might feel emotional the first time, but over time, you lose the emotion.

The point is that nerves are normal and natural. They mean you have landed on an emotion, and they are good.

WHAT CAN I DO TO DEAL WITH MY NERVES?

I get this question all the time, and I usually say, "Let's go over your first line again and again until you nail it."

You can memorize your first line and know it inside and out. You know exactly how you're starting, so that no matter what happens, however freaked out you are, you have that anchor. From there, most people are usually fine.

What we've realized more than anything is how intuitive this whole process is.

Once the first line is nailed, you can relax into speaking your truth and your emotion. You don't need coaching on the rest. Nail the first line and let yourself go the rest of the way.

Also, what I always tell speakers at events is that anxiety and excitement are the same emotion with a different frame.

Anxiety is an excitement but with a negative frame. You're anxious about the outcome. You're anxious about looking good. You're anxious about what people are going to think.

But that same energy can be reframed as excitement. You can be excited about finally letting your truth out into the world. About possibly helping someone else. About seeing what happens once you get this off your chest.

You're nervous because you care. That's great. See your nerves as excitement and you'll be able to deal with them.

SHOULD I FOCUS ON HAVING FUN? WILL THAT HELP?

I don't connect with the phrase "have fun" that much

anymore. It's just something we say all the time, like, "Hey, go play soccer, John, and have fun!"

Having fun is great, but it's just something we say.

Some people aren't going to have fun; they won't know how.

And for most people, this process is not fun.

What you can do is **accept the challenge** and enjoy the accomplishment of speaking your truth.

Rob Friend's story is a great example. He felt like he had lost everything when he got that final concussion and realized he'd never play soccer at that level again. After he gave his talk, he said, "I never thought I could get that feeling back."

This wasn't my goal in inviting him, but the talk was for him—like the feeling he got in the locker room before games.

Some people really do enjoy the process. Ultimately, it's up to you where you go with it. For example, don't be afraid to bring a bit of humor into it. You could even get a little self-deprecating, like joking about suicide, "You people are sick."

It's different than self-judgment because it's lighthearted and makes people laugh. And that can diffuse so much tension in the room in the context of your own story.

Don't be afraid to laugh on the stage. Allow people to laugh at you or with you.

Just don't be making jokes, like, "A nun walks into the bar..." None of that.

CRYING

A lot of people ask, "How do I do this without crying?" This is a big one for people. If it's just a matter of speaking through the tears, then it's not an issue. Yes, you may cry, but no, I've never had a speaker not be understood or not able to continue.

What I see more often when I get this question is that the speaker wants to tell their story, but they don't want to be real.

Of course, if they're going to break down, they may not be quite ready to tell their story. I want people to stay with it long enough beforehand. I don't want them to ever feel pressure.

A lot of people apologize for crying. "I'm sorry, I'm sorry," they say.

What they're really saying is, "I'm sorry for taking up oxygen. I'm sorry for existing."

But I tell people not to try to craft a talk that gets you on and off the stage without crying. You can't hide and tell the story in the same way.

If you need to cry, then cry.

I don't want people apologizing for crying. If they do, they'll be apologizing 50 years from now for not showing up in the world.

If you cry, you cry.

If you laugh, you laugh.

It's simply an emotional expression of who you are.

Don't try to control the emotional outcome.

SHARING WITH SO MANY PEOPLE

One Last Talk is not about getting on a stage and sharing with 150 people or sharing with the world. It's about sharing with at least one person. Let me say this again, to be very clear:

You don't have to do your talk publicly, or speak at the One Last Talk event, or anything like that to be successful with this process.

This is about uncovering your truth and then sharing it with at least one other person on this earth. That's it.

If you want to go further, then do it. But you don't have to.

4.5

What if Well-Intentioned Family and Friends Try to Talk Me Out of It?

Let's say you have this book, and you're really going deep. And you decide, *I'm going to share this with my wife.*

Your wife might say, "I didn't know this was so deep. Why are you sharing this with me? And you're thinking about sharing it in front of your family, or your team, or the world? Why would you do that?"

Even well-intentioned family and friends go right to, "What will people think?"

That's the downside of bringing this to those who are close to you if they are not at the same level of growth as you are.

Until recently, I was the one who wanted to grow, and my wife didn't. So, I was putting her under pressure. I used the analogy of heading up a mountain. I would think, *I'm heading up this mountain, whatever it is. I'm going to dig in and do the things I don't necessarily want to do, but need to do, to better myself.*

As I headed up the mountain, I realized there was a kind of pull from the bottom. So, I would try to come back down and pick her up and carry her up the mountain.

If that didn't work, I would try to push her up the mountain, even if she was kicking and screaming.

But none of that works.

Eventually, I'd go back up the mountain and stay there. That's where we get stuck. We get resentful. We get bitter.

Or sometimes we give up and come down the mountain and say, "You know what? I'm just going to sit here."

A lot of us are afraid of moving up the mountain because we can't see our partner. We feel the gap literally growing. When I use this analogy and give this charge, people say, "Oh my God, this is us."

Eventually, I just had to let my wife go, in a sense. I had to move on and say, "If she's not willing to come, that's okay." So, I turned and went up the mountain, and I didn't peek over my shoulder. When I did turn to look back, I saw her there, taking her first step, leaning in.

It wasn't because I wanted her to.

It was because she wanted to.

The reason I wanted her to grow all that time was because I loved her and saw so much more potential in her.

But she interpreted that as me wanting her to change.

She thought, *If you want me to change, you're basically saying you don't love me for who I am. You love me for who you want me to be. What's wrong with me now?*

So there's a very fine line between growth and change, especially in the context of marriage.

I had to realize that she wouldn't grow until I let her go.

This is a massive problem, especially in marriages. One person is on the growth curve and the other person is not. Kenton Ho spoke about this in his One Last Talk.

He came to an event in Ireland, and when he got back, he was much more genuine, not trying to be somebody else.

But he got massive resistance from his wife, to the point that divorce was on the table. She even left the house one night.

And she hated me.

So, I got on the phone with her one day and said, "How are you doing?"

She said, "Not that great."

I said, "What's going on?"

She said, "I'm just really angry, and I'm losing my husband."

I said, "Before you get into how you're angry and how I'm the bad guy, what are you seeing in him?"

She said, "Things have changed."

"What have you seen change in him?" I asked.

She answered, "He's more confident. He's making better decisions. He's taking more time off. He's looking after himself more. He's more connected to the children. He's happier."

This is actually what she said.

I said, "Okay. And in relation to you?"

She said, "He doesn't need me as much. He doesn't ask for my counsel as much."

So, it was really all about her—controlling and wanting to be the center of attention. I said, "You're describing some things that most people would love."

She said, "Yeah, so annoying. So fucking happy."

She was so angry and bitter. I was asking her about coming to a couple's retreat, and she said, "No, I'm not gonna go. I'm not going to that fucking event."

By the end of the call, I got her to admit two things:

1. These changes in Kenton were good, and
2. Her issues were about her and her resentment—not about him.

Once we worked through this, she calmed down and actually decided to come.

When we got to the couple's retreat, I asked the group,

"Is there anybody here even though they don't want to be? Does anybody feel like they've been pushed here?"

A few hands went up.

I said, "I don't see anybody handcuffed to the chair. But I understand some of you might be here because your spouse has kind of pushed you to be here. It's not because they see something wrong with you and want you to change. It's because they are taking a weekend out of their life to spend it with you to address things the right way, and maybe address things that are taking you off course slightly that will affect you later down the road. How much do they love you to put that kind of value on you?"

I looked over at Kenton's wife, and she was bawling. From that second forward, I couldn't separate the two of them. She was literally sitting there, holding him. I was thinking, *Get a room, you two!*

It's like a lot of mothers. They want their kids to need them and for them to not move away, because that's their identity. They lose who they are when their children leave.

So, when you bring the one last talk to family and friends, you have to be aware of these factors.

Here's what it boils down to:

A lot of family and friends who are close to you want you to be happy—they just don't want you to change.

The reason is because they take it personally. Because it threatens them and their decisions about their life.

If you are growing and changing and improving, what does it mean for them? I'm not saying they should think this way—I am just saying that many people do.

We saw this when we chose to not christen our kids.

We had the bollocks to do something different. And people close to us attacked us because it was different than their decision.

It's hard for people to say, "Good for you. It's not for me, but good for you." It's easier to just attack. Then you don't have to ask yourself whether you made the right decision. You can preserve your ego if you attack.

So, when you share your One Last Talk with somebody in your family, they might criticize it. They might say something like, "Oh my God, you're going to share that dad is an alcoholic? What is he going to say? You can't say that in public."

Inevitably, you'll end up going to those people because you

want them to hear you, because they haven't heard you for years. You want them to hear your pain and validate you. But if those are your reasons, don't share your talk with those people.

I know it seems crazy, right? Why would your family not want you to change?

They don't want you to change because they often see your change as a reflection on them. It forces them to question their own individual journey. Your changes force them to recognize how they're not changing.

The story I share with couples is about one night years ago when my wife came home and wanted to watch a movie. But then she said, "No, the laundry needs to be done."

I said I didn't mind it not being done. She started yelling and was pissed, which isn't normal for her. I said I would look after it, and she said, "You'll do it?"

I again said I would look after it, and she said, "So you'll get somebody else to do it?"

I said, "You're damn right. I've never hung a bleeding church dress, and I never will. Number one is that I'm shitty at doing it. And number two is that my time is way too valuable to be ironing some stupid shirt."

We argued a bit more, and eventually I said, "Forget about it. Sit down, watch the movie, and relax. I'll organize the ironing."

She said, "No, no, no."

I said, "What is really bothering you?"

She talked about how things should be ironed, and we went back and forth on that.

Let's just say that we got somebody in to do the ironing and cleaning in the house.

It all came out when I asked my wife, "Who would be the one person in the world you would hate to find this out?"

She said, "My mom."

The real problem was that she didn't want to be seen as a snob or somebody with money. She needed to play small around her mom. She wanted her mom to continue to love her for who she was. She didn't want to change things, because she thought her family would see it as a negative reflection on their existence and their identity.

But she had to let go of the expectations, primarily unspoken, of the people from home to have a better connection with them. She had to live her own life.

Another example is, when I wrote my first book, I posted something on Facebook about it. I got really positive comments from people in Russia, America, and Canada. They'd say, "Incredible. Great job." The one comment I got from my homeland of Ireland was:

"Don't get too big for your boots."

This is a bigger problem than you might imagine, because it's not just about delivering what you have to say, one-on-one, as a kind of test run for talks. This goes wider.

What if someone hears the talk, or hears about the talk afterwards? What are they going to say?

Even though many One Last Talks have offended family members, I've also seen them open up incredible dialogues and push new boundaries.

You might be still afraid to actually share your One Last Talk because of this. You might still be too concerned about what your family or friends will think. That might just be too consuming for you to move forward with.

If that is the case for you, then I can only tell you this:

Fine. Don't do it.

You keep hiding from your truth and see how that works out for you.

I don't want to lecture on this or come down hard on you if that is your fear. I understand that fear deeply, because I was in that space for 37 years of my life. I came from a culture that has perfected shaming; it's almost an art form for Irish Catholics, so I have sympathy for that view.

I will just invite you to think about this: if you are saying, "I can't speak my truth because it'll offend somebody," then what you are really saying is that you don't matter. That your truth does not matter, and that it's okay to lie and pretend and bullshit everybody in your life—including yourself—in order to perpetuate that.

But SPEAKING THE TRUTH is the thing that people need to do to actually set themselves free, and it's the thing they need to connect with other human beings.

The idea that I can't speak my truth because of what people will think? Personally, I will reject that forever.

If that's the world you live in, then you don't have a chance to be authentic and live a meaningful life.

4.6

Give Your One Last Talk

If you're here—if you did all the exercises and all the work to get here—first off:

Congratulations. I'm proud of you.

It is not easy to get here. To face your truth and commit to speaking it out loud. Take a moment to congratulate yourself.

Just a reminder that will help you if you are still feeling anxious: *this is not just about you.*

There's somebody out there somewhere who has suffered what you have suffered and has gone through what you went through, but most importantly, they are sitting in it right NOW. If you can get back to that core and remind yourself that somebody is exactly where you were, that changes the energy.

You can use your pain for a purpose: to help others get through their pain.

Maybe it's Peggy from Yellowknife.

Maybe it's someone who suffered from sexual abuse and the shame is destroying them.

Maybe it's someone dealing with weight issues.

Maybe it's someone who can't connect with their family.

It could be anyone. You can't know until you step up and give your talk.

But what I can promise you is that there is SOMEBODY you can help with this talk.

You didn't have help when you were going through it, but maybe you can be that person for them.

Even if you cannot do this for you, do it for them.

Now go deliver it. We're all with you.

LAST-MINUTE INSPIRATION

If you need some last-minute inspiration, here are some real testimonials from people who attended One Last Talk events. These are not from speakers. These are only from attendees, and they were all unsolicited. I am putting them here so you can see how important your talk is and to help you really move past any last resistance:

> *I wanted to extend an overdue but heartfelt thank you for the experience you've given me at One Last Talk. I truly took home the impact it had on me. The people I met are absolutely beautiful. Everyone has given me an important lesson: I don't need to follow the unspoken rules of getting a mainstream education, becoming financially free, then finally doing what I truly love. I don't need to wait to check-mark those off until I start exploring my passions and following my dreams.*
>
> *I don't need to wait. I will start today.*

———

> *It's just so great to know that adults have problems too. I don't feel so alone anymore.*

———

> *This was a truly moving event that opened up deep wells*

of emotion for me. I related to each one of the speakers in a different way, and I found that many new paths for self-reflection presented themselves during and after this event. I left feeling full of love and compassion for all those around me, which is probably the greatest feeling on earth.

It helped me own how real or unreal I am being in the presence of my life. To ask questions of myself in regard to the life I'm choosing to live.

Thank you so much for that.

———

My biggest takeaway was the deep relief that my fears and struggles in life are human experiences shared by so many others. I am not alone, and I feel inspired to continue to share my story with others around me.

———

Amazing event! The speakers had a greater impact on me than all the so-called professional speakers I have listened to in my entire life.

———

I had no idea the impact One Last Talk would have on me.

A flood of something is happening, and at this moment in time I cannot stop it, and I'm sure that it's something that shouldn't be stopped...and actually I don't want it to stop. I think I need to sit in my shit! I just wanted to say thanks, as this has had a huge impact on me. I was so impressed and inspired by the honesty, openness, and genuine interest from everyone who attended.

This weekend, I felt things for the first time in my life, and I am overwhelmed with feelings and epiphanies like I've never experienced before. I've been humbled and reminded of how misaligned I've allowed myself to become. I'm so excited to start making decisions for myself for the first time in my life, and to feel the freedom I've always wanted but that I so often blamed others for, when it was really my fault.

I haven't been honest, and I owe that to everyone I love, to start—but most importantly, to myself.

Those people I admire so much, who glow and have endless energy—those unicorns in this world who aren't wearing masks and have worked very hard to find their true meaning—they are the most honest people in this world, and that's what I want to be too.

I can't believe how heavy the stories in this world are, but within those stories are our gifts. We connect through our stories, and we help others. The only way we can connect is when we share them, and that's what we need more of.

———

Personally, I have been struggling with moving forward in my life, and I found myself processing my One Last Talk the night following the event. I got a huge piece of the block and am excited to see what's next.

———

Now go give your talk. We're all with you.

PART

I DID IT—
WHAT'S
NEXT?

FIVE

My One Last Talk Is Done—Now What?

Once you're done delivering your talk, everything in your life should become perfect.

Ha!

I'm kidding, of course.

But buried in that joke is the truth of what should ideally happen after your One Last Talk.

Your life definitely won't become perfect, but it should shift you, and I hope it will shift you in a very important way:

You will now be better equipped and more willing to speak your truth in all aspects of your life.

Let me be clear: speaking your truth will not always be pleasant.

But I believe it is the only way to live—to be fully present and authentic in your life.

The next two chapters show you two different endings to speaking your truth.

In the first, my wife Pauline writes about what happened when she spoke her truth about her rape. It was not the ending she'd hoped for, in many ways, but you'll see why she is still so glad she did it.

In the second, what we call the "movie endings," I go through some of the "Where are they now?" stories from other people who did their One Last Talks.

5.2

The Painful Ending

WRITTEN BY PAULINE MCKERNAN

I did my One Last Talk early on. It was about growing up with a scarcity mindset and the impact that that had on my life—how I make decisions running from what I didn't want as opposed to really focusing on what I wanted. That was kind of the gist of it.

I went as far as I could at the time. But afterwards, I kind of felt that I could've shared more.

I felt like I could've been more vulnerable and shared more of my story. There was something much deeper that I needed to share, that I did not let out.

I eventually shared this deep truth with Philip. I am sure

you can guess what happened: he was like a starving dog with a bone.

He wouldn't let it go. I mean that in the most loving way possible, because he really does mean well, but he is relentless when it comes to this stuff.

It took me a while, but finally I decided to open up and share this deeper truth with some of the people closest to me. Just Philip, some friends, and some family.

It went very well, and I felt better.

But I needed to go further. I needed to share this publicly, with everyone in my life.

I would have done it in a One Last Talk, but we didn't have one scheduled for quite a while, and I wanted—I needed—to share this before then.

I am not on social media, so Philip agreed to post this on his Facebook page, since we share so many of the same friends:

> *My wife was raped, and the impact stays with her to this day. She finally shared this with a couple of people in her life a few years back (including me), but has mostly stayed silent on the story and its grip on her.*

Last month, she agreed to share her story in a book I'm writing to help others. For her courage, I salute her and the many women who are part of the #MeToo movement.

And in case anyone is wondering why I am sharing this, Pauline is not on social media that much and gave me permission to share a part of her story in the hope that it helps someone else tell theirs.

No, it's not the same as a One Last Talk, but it is very much the same core idea: I was sharing a deep, painful truth that I had held in for too long, and I needed to get it out of me.

It's perfectly normal to give a One Last Talk that goes as far as you can at the time, and then want to do another one that goes further later. It happened to me.

But that's not why I am writing this. Philip asked me to write this because of what happened after I shared my truth.

Earlier in the book, Philip talked about how your well-meaning family and friends might try to stop you from sharing your truth in a One Last Talk, and why that happens.

I've seen a lot of people give some very emotionally difficult talks, and for the most part, their friends and family—even the ones who told them not to give the talk— wholeheartedly supported them afterwards.

Many were even inspired to do their own talks, as you've seen. That's usually the way it works.

But that's not *always* the way it works.

Sometimes, you can courageously speak your truth...and your family will reject you for it. By the words they use or by their silence.

In fact, that exact thing happened to me.

Before Philip posted about my rape, I was terrified.

I was afraid of what people would think.

I was afraid that I would be labeled.

I didn't want people's pity. I didn't even want to think about it. I just wanted to cover it up and pretend it didn't happen and make it go away.

Almost as soon as Philip shared that Facebook post, I was swarmed with love and support from our friends. I have to admit, I was very surprised at the overwhelming and loving support that I received from all these people.

And I was even more surprised at how it helped people. People contacted us and told us about the same thing happening to them. They thanked me for sharing it and told us how it helped them face their truth and even share their truth with people in their lives. That was great.

I know I felt relief. I felt lighter as a person as soon as I shared that. I was glad that I did it, as painful as it was, and I was happy that, by sharing my pain, I was able to help other people.

What was very interesting about the whole thing was that I didn't get the support from family that I expected.

Now, I have to admit, I did not talk about this with my family ahead of time. I had told two of my sisters the previous year. However, the rest of my family did not know this happened to me. My two sisters that had known about it did not know I'd be putting it out to the world.

And yes, putting it on Facebook was possibly not the best way to announce it to the world. It might have been better to talk to them first. However, I was inspired to do it one evening and just did it.

But that is also kind of the point: this is my truth—not anyone else's. I can speak my truth the way I choose, where I choose.

My sister started texting me saying, "Hey, you ought to tell mom and dad" (my parents are not on Facebook, they don't even have a computer).

So, I called her, and told her that I would call them. And much to my surprise, she was very cross with me on the phone, saying things like, "Now I have to pick up the pieces." Then she changed course, and told me not to tell them, that it would "kill them."

I became a nervous wreck. After a few days of contemplation, I decided, *Okay, I'm going to tell them,* and I decided to call my parents. However, just as I was about to call them my mother called me. She had got a phone call from a friend with the "news."

Understandably she was upset; however, most of the phone call was around how she found out and why I didn't tell her at the time—that she must be a bad mother. She couldn't understand why I was telling people now. She was really cross with Phillip. She was really cross that it was going to be in a book. She was concerned about my kids and how they would feel. And she would not stop going on and on about how she heard, why talk about it now, why bring up the past, and how many people knew, and that sort of thing.

I felt from the conversation that I had to defend myself, I

felt ashamed and spent most of the phone call apologizing. It only occurred to me afterwards that I had felt guilty for most of the call, hence my apologies. In my mind, that conversation validated why I didn't tell anyone in the first place.

The more I thought about this, the angrier I got.

I called her back a few days later, and I think she had felt that the last call had been the end of conversation, because she started the conversation as though nothing had happened: "Oh, how's the weather?" that kind of thing.

I wanted to find out who called her to let her know that I was raped; however, she would not tell me and told me she'd never tell me.

I still do not know who called her and told her, and the subject of my rape has never been mentioned again.

What did I expect?

You know, I guess I kind of hoped that it would maybe open some conversations. Bring us together as a family.

And it may yet do that.

As I write that, I feel like a hypocrite. I would like open

conversations, yet I didn't tell my family my deepest darkest secret.

There is massive learning opportunity in this for me as well around my expectations and desires of others, and I ask myself: "Do I do the very thing that I expect and want from people?"

That is one of the most beneficial things for me in this whole process. It's not that my family let me down. It's framing the right question: How do I want to live? How do I want to communicate with my kids and husband, and as an extension, those closest to me?

I now choose to speak my truth—to step into conversations with as much honesty and love as I can muster.

Sadly, I think a lot of people who want to speak a painful truth, through One Last Talk or another way, are facing a situation similar to this.

And I think it stops many people from speaking that truth. Or if they do, it makes a difficult situation harder, like in my case.

That's why I was also willing to talk about this for the book. Because I think some people will prepare their One Last

Talk, and they will know what they want to say, but they will face some kind of pressure and resistance.

And they may hesitate on giving their talk because of this pressure.

So why now? Why share?

I was tired of keeping this secret.

I kind of felt like a bit of a phony.

Here I was, giving a One Last Talk, married to a man who has dedicated his life to helping people speak their truth, and this is my truth, and I was holding it in.

Further and more importantly for me, I believe not speaking about my rape has resulted in my inability to share about so many things in life. I kept quiet about so many things, and now I'm tired of it.

I'm not happy that I upset my parents, but you know, it was time someone in my family spoke up about how they actually feel.

I hope that my parents and family can get beyond that. I don't think our relationship will be the same, and that's actually fine, because I think it needs to change, and I want it to change, and I believe it can change.

While this process has been painful for me, there is hope and beauty beyond that. As I mentioned earlier, I am really questioning how I want to show up in the world. But more than that, I feel better personally.

My relationship with myself is much better. I am so much more confident and courageous and just...calm.

I feel like such a better version of myself. I feel lighter, and I can honestly say that I underestimated the impact of not sharing my story.

I believe it held me back in so many ways—in building relationships where I'd hold back and not fully commit, almost like building a hard exterior wall around myself. I'd put everyone in front of myself. In essence, I was scarce with myself.

On the other hand, sharing what I went through has lifted a massive weight off me. I fully embrace every part of me, and I am okay with it.

For example, I used to look in the mirror at my body and think, *Ugh*...Now I look and say, *Yeah, pretty good for a 45-year-old.*

My relationship with my husband and my children has never been better. Even though the kids don't know (I don't plan to tell them until they are of a proper age), it helped our relationship. I am now able to show up more fully with them because I am showing up fully for myself.

And the support I received from family and friends and extended community was incredible, and so appreciated.

I am not here to tell you what to do. I just wanted to share my story—to help you understand what might happen—so you can make the right decision for yourself about sharing your truth.

5.3

The Movie Ending

Here are some updates on some of the lives of the One Last Talk speakers you read about in these pages. This is just to give you an idea of the impact speaking your truth has on your life:

BEV:

I've been struggling for a couple of weeks now with how to convey my utmost gratitude and appreciation for One Last Talk. It's just too huge.

How do you adequately thank someone who helped you move from numb acceptance to vibrant feeling?

How do you thank someone for helping you move from dull existence to excited anticipation?

How do you thank someone who helped you move from self-loathing to self-love and then translate that into unconditional love for others?

I can't figure it out. Piles of crumbled paper, walks in the woods, meditating, and just trying very hard haven't worked.

But my inability to convey the depth of my thanks, gratitude, and appreciation does not stop me from at least saying a very heartfelt thank you.

BRIAN:

I can say, with conviction, that One Last Talk has fundamentally changed my life.

When Phillip asked me to speak, I was excited to share what I call the Five Fs. I was in the middle of writing my book about these truths, and that was what I was sure I wanted to share. Then Philip posed the question to me, "Brian, if you knew you were going to die tomorrow, what gift do you want to leave your children?"

I immediately shifted the focus of my One Last Talk to self-love and forgiveness.

Writing my One Last Talk was very hard. It forced me

to open up and share this all with my wife. She, in turn, opened up to me about some things from her past I was not aware of, and our level of communication and marriage/ friendship went to another level.

My father flew with me to Vancouver to hear my One Last Talk and had no idea of the abortions and trouble I got myself into. I remember being filled with such anxiety and not being able to sleep a wink the night before the event, for fear of how my father would react. I so much wanted his acceptance and forgiveness and unconditional love as any child does.

As soon as my talk ended, my father asked for the micro-phone in a room full of 200+ strangers and said to me, "Son, I love you and am so proud of you. I only hope your two young boys grow up to be the man you are someday."

Needless to say, this experience melted me. Those words changed the trajectory of our friendship and respect for one another. My relationship with my father is now deeper than it's been in 44 years of living.

Most importantly, my relationship with myself changed. It's now one of mostly joy and gratitude, which continues to grow through that healthy internal relationship. And the external relationships that matter most to me have gone deep in a way I did not know existed before, with my family, friends, and other loved ones.

In preparing my One Last Talk, the entire front half of my book shifted and changed and opened me up to share my message with the world, which I continue to do today. My book (What Matters Most), which refers a lot to that OLT experience, has allowed me to continue to share my message on stage and through my book all over the world.

I am still amazed at how many people will come to me and open up about some dark things from their past that they have buried and not forgiven themselves for.

One woman in particular approached me after a talk who appeared to be 70+ years old, with tears in her eyes. We embraced, and she told me that she had had an abortion when she was a teenager some 50+ years ago and had buried that experience, and she now has given herself permission to forgive and see it as an opportunity to grow versus a crisis.

This one experience alone is testament to the impact that One Last Talk has and will continue to have as a global movement for the things that matter most in life. I am honored to be a part of Phillip's book, and he continues to be a mentor and great friend, and I look forward to watching One Last Talk grow.

ROB FRIEND:

One Last Talk had a tremendous impact on me. I met Philip after my injury. I was in a transitional period in my life, and One Last Talk really helped bring my struggle and reality to light. The fact was, I was in denial. I pretended that my life was great, playing golf every day, doing nothing, but in reality, it kind of sucked.

One Last Talk woke me up and shook me and made me re-engage my life. It helped me see that I was avoiding facing my reality, that I was in transition and that was OK. And most importantly, it helped me refocus and begin to search for answers to the most important questions about my life; namely, what do I want to do now?

After One Last Talk, I identified areas I wanted to pursue. Real estate was one, and I found I was passionate about that. I now have a very successful real estate company.

I also realized that I still loved soccer, even if I couldn't do it professionally. I could still coach, and teach, and facilitate soccer for others. As part of this realization, I opened an indoor soccer facility in Vancouver. It's the largest one in the city.

I also decided to help my country create their own professional soccer league. Can you believe Canada is the only developed nation in the world without a pro soccer league? Not anymore.

I joined up with a team of great people, and we started the Canadian Premier League, so Canadians can play pro soccer without having to leave their country, like I did. And I own a team, Pacific FC Van Isle.

I doubt I would have done any of this without doing my One Last Talk. If you are thinking about doing this, I just can't recommend it enough. I know it's scary but go for it.

MATTHEW:

When I was young, nothing made me happier than making my brother laugh so hard his stomach would hurt the next day. Nothing, except repeating this pattern again the following day, while he was still in pain. Admittedly, this pleased me a bit more.

I believe this is what sparked inside of me the desire to write, specifically for tv, even more specifically the genre of comedy.

Problem was, I never felt deserving of doing what made me happy, and I never fully saw the value cracking silly jokes provided in the world, so I subconsciously sabotaged my dreams at every pass. I over-complicated my goals, measured myself against others' success, felt the anxiety of not possessing someone else's voice, and eventually threw in the towel.

That all began to change the day I delivered my One Last Talk.

When I agreed to give my talk in front of what I presumed would be an angry mob brandishing rotten tomatoes in cocked arms ready to release hell upon me as I crumbled into the fetal position center stage, suffice to say I was a tad nervous.

In fact, I don't actually recall why I agreed to give my talk in the first place, as I am deathly afraid of public speaking. Perhaps it was the immense trust I hold in Philip, who believed I needed to do it. Perhaps the pain of hiding from myself and the world had gotten too great.

Whatever the reason, when I took that stage in front of a couple hundred strangers, something unexpected happened:

I wasn't booed, nor did I soil myself.

In fact, the most surprising thing was that I actually received a standing ovation.

Sure, this was great for the ego and confidence, but it ran much deeper than that. I felt as though I had been heard. The real me. I had been accepted. The real me.

In the months that followed, I began to notice some powerful ripple effects as a direct result of delivering my One Last Talk:

- *A close family member opened up to me and trusted me with their own similar experience, which creating a dialogue that didn't exist before.*
- *Multiple friends and family members began being more vulnerable and real around me.*
- *My wife was inspired to write and share with me her own One Last Talk, which helped me to understand her in a new way and connect on a deeper level.*
- *Because I had declared on stage publicly who I was, and more importantly who I wasn't, I noticed that my talk had become a line in the sand for personal alignment and decision making about my future.*
- *I stopped being so apologetic about who I really was and started showing up more in the world, which had a positive effect on my children, especially as they find their own ways in the world.*

And while these are just a few of the many examples, which stand as a testament to the impact delivering my One Last Talk has had on my life and on some of the lives of the people I care most about, there's one more tiny, yet critical, thing that happened that day on stage that is worth mentioning:

While reliving the very moment I tried to take my own life and sharing the details of that moment, I managed to coax a few chuckles out of the crowd, which ignited that tiny little familiar flame inside of me from my childhood.

An innocent little joke seemed to allow the audience to not only digest the potency of that dramatic moment, but to also connect with it, and to me, on some sort of deep, shared level.

After I stepped off that stage, I began to write more of what made me laugh. I began sharing more of what I wrote.

After years of hiding, I had finally found MY voice.

I eventually even wrote a TV pilot which was produced, and I am in the process of securing another TV pilot development deal.

I've come to learn that comedy is an amazing frequency that allows you to go deeper with people, in a way that's welcome. When people laugh, their brain releases more endorphins than just about any drug. It helps them smile, enjoy life, escape something temporarily, and not feel alone. Because when you share a laugh, you feel connected, which means you matter.

In short, I've finally learned the value of comedy: it connects and heals. And through this process of discovery, I also began to unearth the value within myself.

I feel incredibly fortunate to be where I'm at right now in my young writing career. Everything is still new. Everything is still an experiment. Every character I create. Every storyline. Every mistake. It's all part of what makes my voice what it is. It's all part of making me...well, ME.

And it all started because I crafted and delivered my One Last Talk.

QUAN:

When I went up there, it was very hard, but good. To have my mom there and be able to hear the story was so important. That was her first time hearing anything like that. She knew what I went to prison for, but I don't think she was ever able to really hear the whole story in that way.

She said for me to be up there and for her to hear me talking, she suddenly realized that things were not okay in the past, and that she wished that she had been able to be there for me back then. In my culture, you don't talk about it. And she said since I never talked about anything, she always thought everything was okay, and she realized that it wasn't.

And so, I think it was just a tremendous sense of loss for her. She realized what she missed.

There was a huge stigma and shame that her son killed someone, and it was something she never talked about. So I think for me to go up there and talk about it with her and for her to see it, I think she became more accepting of what happened and that it wasn't her fault that she raised me wrong in some way.

At the same time, I think it just made me and her, our relationship, be so much closer. We're just able to enjoy each other's presence more.

My One Last Talk was my first time getting up in front of an audience or on a stage or anything like that, and to share with basically the world this is what I had done. Only my really close friends kind of know what I went to prison for, and even then I don't really get into much detail. I told some of them, but not the extent that I shared at One Last Talk.

And so I think that doing it and feeling still accepted and supported after, it gave me a sense of...I keep saying the word peacefulness but that's just the only way I can describe it. I just felt so at peace with myself, my place in the world, and what I want to do moving forward.

NEELY:

My One Last Talk changed my life in so many ways. The big thing for me is that sometimes I get this overwhelming feeling of pride in myself.

I think people can see the pride in me. The confidence. It's a very warm, satisfying feeling. When I think about it, it's funny, I can feel my posture change. The way I present myself to other people. I think it transcends and transforms. I've become a lot more open. I don't hide as much when I'm around people.

There are some not so nice feelings that came with it too. It's not all rainbows and butterflies after you do this. I've had to have some hard conversation, and I know that there's still some hard things and conversations to come that aren't going to be easy.

But it does make those conversations easier. I feel like I can go into those more gracefully than I would have before in putting myself where I should be.

But some of the conversations it created were amazing. Right afterwards, I started talking with my boyfriend about the impact it had on me. How my one singular incident affected so many people. For a long time, I felt like I was consumed and stuck in my own victim story. It really got me thinking about how to help people step out of that themselves.

I realized that I wanted to start talking to more people about their stories around sexual abuse. Not just the victims. Close family members of victims. Friends of victims. Maybe even other types of people. How it's shown up in their life.

I think people naturally want to turn away from these conversations, whether you're the victim or your closely associated with one. For so many people it's come up since I told my story, that it wasn't necessarily the abuse itself, but it was how your family or the people close to you dealt with it. How that made you feel about yourself.

I want to help them have those conversations. I think that's where the real pain was for me. So helping people understand the real pains in these sexual abuse cases, this became an important thing for me.

I've decided to start a podcast about this. It's about to launch, and I think I will call it "The Head Nod."

That also came from One Last Talk too. All these different people that came up to me after my talk. Two of them told me their story. I might still be the only person who knows. I hope not, but for both, I was the first person they'd ever told.

Some people I could tell wanted to talk to me, but they couldn't. They just gave me a head nod. Kind of like, "Me too. I can't even speak it. I just want you to know" kind of thing.

That killed me, but it also made me feel really good.

It's something for them, for the people who can't even say what happened. It wasn't very long ago that I was the same.

Maybe this podcast will help them unlock it in a way. Maybe they think they have to go through this horrible, deep, dark place to get to where they feel like a normal person again. I think it will be out by the time the book is out.

You know what's funny? Sometimes, I get this vague feeling like I've done something wrong.

And then I catch myself, and I say to myself, "No you didn't do anything wrong. You spoke your truth, and that's never wrong."

And slowly, I am starting to replace that feeling with a

feeling of being so proud of what I did. Every time I think of it I get teary eyed.

I've never felt that way about myself until I did my One Last Talk.

5.4

How to Share Your One Last Talk

By writing and delivering a One Last Talk to another person, you are joining a larger community of people. You are now in a community with Quan and Bev and Neely and all the others who've had the courage to do that.

If you'd like to become more active in this community, possibly even share your One Last Talk with the world, maybe attend a live event, or see the other ways that people are using One Last Talk to help them, head to:

www.onelasttalk.com

We'd love to have you involved in any way that you'd like.

5.5

Life After One Last Talk

Right now, the question you should be asking yourself is very similar to the question that an audience member asked Tucker Max at the end of his One Last Talk:

What are you going to do now? Are you going to keep talking about these things? Please, don't just close this up and put it in a box and bury it in the yard. I for one would love if you allowed us to see that part of you a lot more, because that's what we need.

Please do not just read this book and let it become another book on your bookshelf. There are so many people that read books and say things like, "Oh my god, that book changed my life."

So, I ask them, "Great, how?"

And they say, "Well, because it did."

So I respond, "Yes, I know, but how? Like what did you do as a result? And what are you doing now?"

They often don't have an answer. They're too busy reading the next book, which is also changing their life, but they won't do anything from it.

Don't allow One Last Talk be one of those books. Don't just do it and then you're done and move on with life. That is my ultimate invitation to you:

Once you are done with your first One Last Talk, keep speaking your truth.

Spread your truth to all aspects of your life. Integrate the truth you spoke in your talk into everything you speak and do for the rest of your life. And go further. Go deeper.

This is the only thing that will both keep you alive and keep you living at the same time:

Speak your truth, and then keep speaking it for the rest of your life.

About the Author

When the most successful leaders and entrepreneurs need clarity in their lives they call **PHILIP McKERNAN**. He has coached Olympic Athletes and has consulted with The Pentagon.

Philip helps people get clear on who they are and where they need to go. He helps people transition in their personal and professional lives so they get aligned in all areas of life. Philip does not let his clients hide or lie to themselves. He helps them face the reality they need to get the life they want.

You can learn more about him at PhilipMckernan.com.